. . . from *Mau`i Trails*

The island of Maui is unique in Polynesia: it is the only island named for a deity. Maui was a great mischief-maker, and legends about his escapades (or "strifes") occur throughout Polynesia.

When streams flowing down Puu Kukui's slopes scoured out Iao Valley from the old volcano's softer material, Iao Needle and its ridge withstood the streams' cutting forces. At 2250 feet high, Iao Needle now stands over 1200 feet above the valley floor.

On my latest visit, I enjoyed watching a handsome stilt moving gracefully from hummock to hummock as it hunted, and I chuckled at the antics of a couple of crabby, squabbling mudhens—the phrase "mad as a wet hen" came irresistibly to mind.

Mature amauu fronds are a bright green, while young fronds are a bright red. Together, set against the black rock, they're a sight you'll never forget.

Haleakala's nene aren't thieves, but they're accomplished beggars. If you find them hanging around the cabins and campgrounds in the crater, look out! They'll come running for a handout when you unzip your daypack or pull some trail mix out of your pocket.

Maui Trails

Walks, strolls and treks on the Valley Island

Kathy Morey

 WILDERNESS PRESS · BERKELEY, CA

Maui Trails

1st EDITION 1991
2nd EDITION 1996
3rd EDITION July 2003
2nd printing September 2004

Front cover photo copyright © 2003 by Douglas Peebles
Back cover photo copyright © 2003 by Kathy Morey
Interior photos, except where noted, by Kathy Morey
Maps: © 2003 by Kathy Morey

Library of Congress Card Number 96-6853
ISBN 0-89997-323-X
UPC 7-19609-97323-2

Manufactured in the United States of America

Published by: **Wilderness Press**
1200 5th Street
Berkeley, CA 94710
(800) 443-7227; FAX (510) 558-1696
info@wildernesspress.com
www.wildernesspress.com
Visit our website for a complete listing of our books and for ordering information.

Cover photos: Sandcastle on Wailea Beach, Maui, Hawaii (front);
Silversword and Waimoku Falls, Maui, Hawaii (back)
Frontispiece: Blue Pool, Maui, Hawaii

SAFETY NOTICE: Although Wilderness Press and the author have made every attempt to ensure that the information in this book is accurate at press time, they are not responsible for any loss, damage, injury, or inconvenience that may occur to anyone while using this book. You are responsible for your own safety and health while in the wilderness. The fact that a trail is described in this book does not mean that it will be safe for you. Be aware that trail conditions can change from day to day. Always check local conditions and know your own limitations.

Library of Congress Cataloging-in-Publication Data
Morey, Kathy.
        Maui trails: walks, strolls, and treks on the valley isle / Kathy Morey. —3rd ed.
            p.   cm.
        Includes bibliographical references and index.
        ISBN 0-89997-323-X
        1. Maui (Hawaii) — Guidebooks. 2. Hiking — Maui.
        I. Title
DU628.M3M67   2003
919.69'21 — dc20   96-6853
                                                                            CIP

Dedication

To my husband Ed, with love. Thanks for hiking with me, giving me shuttle rides, reading my manuscripts, and providing honest criticism.

Acknowledgments

I'm deeply grateful to Thomas Winnett, President Emeritus of Wilderness Press, for his encouragement, help, advice, and endless patience. Also, I wish to thank Jaan Hitt, for the beautiful job she did in redesigning the Hawaii series of books, Douglas Peebles who provided the cover photographs, Teddy Hargrove who assisted with the final manuscript preparation, Jannie Dresser, Managing Editor, and Mike Jones, Publisher of Wilderness Press.

My thanks to all the readers who took the time to write me and to give me the benefit of their experience in using this book. I tried to put your information to good use, and I hope it's reflected in the pages of this third edition. Please keep up the good work!

I am very much indebted to Jerry Schad. His use of icons to help summarize hikes in his outstanding *Afoot & Afield* series of hiking guides for Southern California (available from Wilderness Press) inspired me to create and use icons in this series of guides.

Spokespeople for Maui's Division of Land and Natural Resources, for Na Ala Hele, for the Hawaii Nature Center, and for Haleakala National Park were very helpful, too. Thank you.

I'm grateful to another valuable source of information: the people who operated the places where we stayed. They were always ready with plenty of local knowledge and advice.

I hope I have accurately and adequately reflected the information these people provided. Any misunderstandings or errors are my responsibility.

— Kathy Morey

Contents

East Maui Trips

Haleakala Trips

Moa on lava

Butterfly on daisy

Heads Up!

Hiking in any wilderness or backcountry area involves potential risks that every hiker must be aware of and respect. The fact that a trail is described in this book is not a guarantee that it will be safe for you. Trails vary greatly in difficulty and in the degree of conditioning and agility one needs to enjoy them safely. Routes may have changed or conditions may have deteriorated since the descriptions were written, particularly in a climatic zone as volatile as the Hawaiian islands.

Wilderness Press attempts to address these changes with each new edition, but every season, every year, every storm front or weather pattern, has an immediate impact on terrain, thus altering trails and instantly dating the book. A trail that is safe on a dry day or for a highly conditioned, agile, and properly equipped hiker may be completely unsafe and inappropriate for someone less prepared or for an exquisitely prepared hiker who runs into an unpredictably adverse weather condition (such as the hurricanes that devastated Kauai in 1982 and 1992).

Minimize your risks by being knowledgeable, prepared, and alert. Be aware of your limitations and of conditions existing whenever and wherever you hike. If conditions are dangerous, or if you are not prepared to deal with them safely, choose a different hike! It's better to have wasted a drive than to be the subject of a rescue. And, on Maui, no drive is ever truly a waste!

Notes About the Third Edition

Maui Trails was originally published in 1991. With each new edition and new printing, we have corrected and updated the information. For this third edition of *Maui Trails*, we also overhauled the design, improved the maps, and added new photographs, all in response to readers' suggestions. You'll find historical, botanical, geological and other information in interesting sidebars, while your trail description remains a continuous narrative. This lets you use the book to prepare for your hike or as great lunchtime reading as you sit beside a beautiful waterfall or overlook a breathtaking stretch of scenery. My guess is, though, you won't be spending too much time with your nose in this book, and I won't take offense. Enjoy Maui!

Pohuehue

Hana coast

Maui: Overview of Principle Hiking Areas

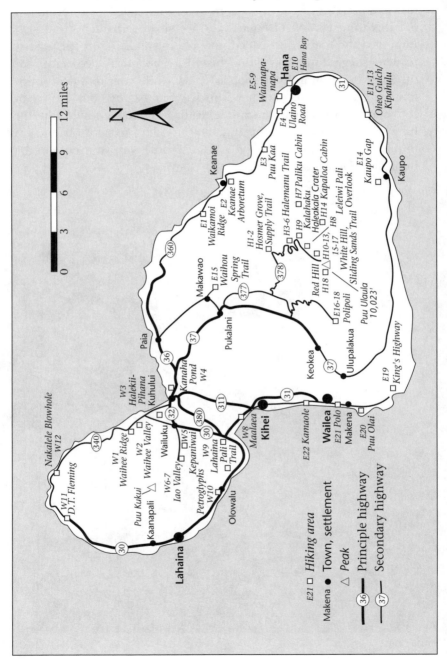

Introduction

"Maui? What do I know about Maui? Nothing! I just own a condo there."

What a shame! Maui is an island of overwhelming beauty and of great contrasts; it defies the mind's attempts to take it all in. It's a large island whose shape, rugged terrain, and road conditions defy the driver's attempts to see it by car. A drive around it or a flight over it may satisfy the eyes, but it denies the other senses their experiences: the fragrance of yellow ginger, the sound of rainforest bamboo rattling in the breeze, the feeling of warm sand underfoot, the sharp taste of wild guavas.

You can't experience Maui fully from a condo or even from a vehicle. The best of the island is outside, along the trails, where there's nothing to separate you from the immediate sensory experience, even sensory overload, of Maui. You don't have to walk far: a worthwhile hike on Maui can be as short as a quarter-mile stroll suitable for anyone who's ambulatory, or it can be as long as a three-day backpack in Haleakala's crater. How do I know? I have walked every trail that is used in this book at least once and most of them twice.

The shape of things

Maui consists of a west lobe and an east lobe connected by an isthmus. Maui's older, smaller, west lobe, West Maui, is a single volcano whose flanks have eroded into deep valleys and knife-thin ridges. Its upper slopes and cloud-covered peak harbor a nearly impenetrable swamp. Maui's younger, much larger east lobe, East Maui, is also a single volcano, Haleakala. On Haleakala's vast flanks are rainforests, huge cattle ranches, parched deserts of jagged lava, and native dryland forests. Erosion has carved immense stream valleys into Haleakala.

1

Two of the largest of those valleys meet atop Haleakala to form what's commonly referred to as Haleakala's "crater."[1] Recently, it's been discovered that glaciation also played a role in shaping Haleakala's "crater" when Haleakala itself was younger and higher—an estimated 15,000 feet rather than its present 10,023 feet—during the most recent ice age. (No matter how it got there, it *is* a crater in the very loose sense of being a big pit at the top of a big mountain.) Long white beaches backed by thorny *kiawe* trees face bays of turquoise water on the drier west and south shores of West and East Maui. The north and east slopes are covered by rainforests and corrugated by steep cliffs and deep gullies. Between West and East Maui lies a low, sandy isthmus where business and industry are concentrated. Broad fields of pineapple and sugarcane carpet the isthmus and the drier slopes of both volcanoes.

Take time for Maui

It takes time to see Maui, partly because there's so much to see and partly because most of the tourist accommodations are far from the major scenic areas (including the best hiking areas). The resorts are concentrated almost exclusively on the west shore of West Maui (Lahaina, Kaanapali, and Kapalua) and on the southwest shore of East Maui (Kihei, Wailea, and Makena). There are some very good hikes scattered near the resorts. However, the only major scenic and hiking area that's "convenient" to the resorts is Iao Valley State Park. The resorts are a *long* way from scenic areas like Haleakala National Park, Hana town and the road to it, and the Oheo Gulch/Kipahulu District of Haleakala National Park.[2]

If you have only a day or two on Maui, stay put and enjoy what's nearby. There's probably a short hike or two in this book that will be very near you. Come back for a longer visit when you can!

---

1 "Crater" implies a volcanic origin to most people. A geologist suggested I refer to Haleakala's most famous feature as its "stream- and glacier-carved valley," but I found that very clumsy and have chosen to stick to "crater."

2 Oheo Gulch Kipahulu was for a time referred to as Seven Sacred Pools," a name that seems to have been a travel promoter's thoughtless invention. There are more than seven pools, and none was ever sacred. The Park Service refers to the area as the Kipahulu District; when I say "Kipahulu," I mean the Kipahulu District of Haleakala National Park. (There's also a tiny Kipahulu village beyond the Kipahulu District of Haleakala National Park.)

If possible, stay a week or two on Maui. Allow at least half a day to visit Iao Valley State Park. Allow a full day to visit Haleakala's summit area; realize that you'll spend about half of it driving. If you want to drive to Hana, plan to stay at least one night in or near Hana, at least two nights if you also wish to visit Kipahulu.[3] Backpackers will probably want to spend three nights—the maximum allowed in any 30-day period—in Haleakala's crater, though three nights (or, rather, the four days around them) are barely enough to see the entire crater.

Be a good visitor

Traffic and crowding near resort and urban areas can be as bad as on the mainland. Developers in resort areas are bulldozing the wild, natural Maui into a tame, plastic Maui almost faster than Maui natives can get out of the way. Local people may (understandably) worry that if they stand still too long, they'll be 'dozed, too. In these areas, even in once remote Hana, the *aloha* spirit seems tattered. Hawaii is not Paradise. Paradise is infinite and self-renewing. Hawaii is a real place of finite space and resources, where real people live real lives with jobs, families, budgets, and bills. Hawaii needs loving care from its visitors as well as from its natives. As the number of tourists increases, I think it becomes important that we visitors actively contribute to the *aloha* spirit instead of just passively expecting to receive it. Bring your best manners and your patience with you to Maui. Be the first to smile and wave. Be the first to pull your car over (safely) so that someone else can pass. Be scrupulous in observing the rules of the trail in order to help preserve what's left of Maui's vanishing wild places. NO TRESPASSING, KEEP OUT, or KAPU ("forbidden") signs mean, "You stay out." Please respect those signs.

---

3 A few tourist accommodations, including budget accommodations in Hana, exist outside the resort areas. See J.D. Bisignani's *Hawaii Handbook* (in the Bibliography) for more information—though the prices may be out of date. Bed-and-breakfast accommodations exist, too. See also Appendix A, Camping on Maui, in this book.

Hiking on the Valley Isle

The search for the perfect trail guide

I wish I could be certain this is a flawless book. However, some things limit an author's ability to produce a perfect, error-free, always up-to-date book. Here are some of the factors, and what you can do to help yourself (and me).

Nature makes constant revisions; so do agencies. Nature constantly reshapes the landscape across which we plan to trek. That's usually a gradual process, but once in a while she makes drastic changes overnight. A landslide can erase a trail in seconds. Erosion can undercut a cliff edge and make last year's safe hike an extremely dangerous one, so that the local authorities close a trail you'd hoped to ramble on. And Maui's fragile volcanic terrain erodes quite rapidly.

Agencies in charge of hiking areas may close an area because they've realized it's environmentally too sensitive to withstand more human visits. An area once open to overnight camping may become a day-use-only area. Trails become impassable from lack of maintenance. Happily, agencies may open new areas because they've been able to acquire new acreage or complete a trail-building project.

Change is the only thing that's constant in this world, so that guidebook authors and publishers always play "catch up" with Nature and with agencies. We want to keep guidebooks up to date, but we are always at least one step behind the latest changes. The day when you'll have constantly revised books on-line at your wristwatch/computer terminal isn't here yet. So it's possible that a few trail descriptions are becoming obsolete even as this book goes to press.

Write for the latest information

It's a good idea to use this book in conjunction with the latest information from the agency in charge of the areas that you plan to hike in. However, this book gives you a far more complete and detailed picture of Maui's principal hiking and backcountry camping opportunities than the current recreation map does. And it describes those opportunities from a hiker's perspective.

Still, it's a good idea to write to these agencies as soon as you've read this book and decided where you want to hike and camp on Maui. Ask them for their latest trail and camping maps, regulations, and permit-issuing procedures. Except for Haleakala National Park, enclose a stamped, self-addressed envelope for your convenience in getting the information you need as soon as possible. (National parks almost always use the franking privilege of Federal agencies, so you'd be wasting a stamp.) Their addresses and telephone numbers are listed below in "Getting Permits or Permission."

Prepare yourself with general information, too

A generous source of useful information about Hawaii is the Hawaii Visitors Bureau. You'll find it at (800) GO-HAWAI as well as on the World Wide Web at www.visit.hawaii.org, a site that offers colorful pages including "Vacation Planner" pages for the State of Hawaii and for each major island. For a vacation planner specific to Maui, call (800) 525-MAUI or (800) 525-6284.

To reach Hawaii Visitors Bureau regional offices contact them in these locations:

> **Canada:** affiliates Nick Hughes and Barbara Newton, 1260 Hornby St., #104, Vancouver, BC V6Z 1W2, (604) 669-6691, FAX (604) 683-9114
> **New York:** in the Empire State Building at 350 Fifth Avenue, Suite 1827, New York, NY 10118, (212) 947-0717, FAX (212) 947-0725
> **Washington, D.C.:** 3975 University Drive, Suite 335, Fairfax, VA 22080, (703) 691-1800, FAX (703) 691-4820

Check out the following Web sites and their links, too:
> **Hawaii Visitors Bureau sites:** www.visit.hawaii.org,
> www.gohawaii.com
>
> **Hawaii State Government offices:** www.hawaii.gov
>
> **Division of Land and Natural Resources (DLNR):**
> www.hawaii.gov/dlnr/
>
> **DLNR, Division of Forestry:** www.hawaii.gov/dlnr/dfw/dfw.html
>
> **DLNR, Division of State Parks:** www.hawaii.gov/dlnr/dsp/dsp.html
>
> **State Tourism office:** www.hawaii.gov/tourism/index.html
>
> **Haleakala National Park:** www.nps.gov/hale/
>
> **Great Outdoors Recreation Pages (GORP):** www.gorp.com—lots of
> info as well as an on-line bookstore

To see some of your hikes in advance as well as to read about them here, get the video trail guide *Pathways in Paradise: Maui*. If your outdoor or travel store doesn't carry the video, you can find it on the Web via the on-line bookstore at the Great Outdoors Recreation Pages (www.gorp.com). It includes coverage of a new trail, the Lahaina Pali Trail. Call the Hawaiian trail organization, Na Ala Hele, at (808) 871-2521 for more information.

Getting permits or permission

The trip descriptions in this book include information about what permits you need (if any) and to whom you should apply for them. A few interesting dayhikes are on private property. This section gives the addresses and telephone numbers of private parties you must apply to for permission to hike in those areas. As of this writing, the government agencies—federal, state, and county—don't require you to have permits in order to *dayhike* on Maui in areas under their jurisdiction (Haleakala National Park does require permits for backpacking; see Appendix A). For completeness, this section also includes the addresses and telephone numbers of the government agencies, as you may want to write or call them for more information. Appendix A in this book gives you detailed information about camping—car camping, tent camping, and cabins—including permit requirements, fees, etc.

Waihee Valley hike (Wailuku Agribusiness)

You must get a permit *in person* for this hike (Trip W2) from Wailuku Agribusiness, (808) 244-9570. Call ahead to find out their current hours. They're in Waikapu, a community 2 miles south of Wailuku on Highway 30. As you approach Waikapu, look for Waiko Road, also signed as Highway 305. It's just north of the bridge over

Waikapu Stream; it may be marked by a blue-and-white sign that points along it to the Waikapu Community Center. Turn east onto Waiko Road and follow it 0.5 mile to a stop sign. Turn left at this inter-section and then almost immediately left again into Wailuku Agribusiness's parking lot. Go into the office to apply. Permits are issued only *on* the day of your hike if it's a weekday. For a weekend or holiday hike, you can get permits in advance on Friday or the last busi-ness day before the holiday.

Haleakala National Park

No permits are required to dayhike or car camp in Haleakala National Park. Backpacking in the crater, including camping or use of the cabins in the crater, requires permits; see Appendix A in this book. For more information, write or call:

> Haleakala National Park
> Box 369
> Makawao, Maui, HI 96768
> (808) 572-4400
> www.nps.gov/hale/

Division of State Parks

No permits are required to hike in Maui's state parks, and none is big enough for or equipped for backpacking. Car camping and use of the cabins do require permits; see Appendix A in this book. For more information, write or call:

> Department of Land and Natural Resources
> Division of State Parks, Maui District
> 54 South High Street, Suite 101
> Wailuku, Maui, HI 96793
> (808) 984-8109
> www.hawaii.gov/dlnr/dsp/dsp.html

If you need to see them in person, they are currently in Wailuku in the State Office Building at 54 High Street, on the southeast corner of Highway 30 (Honoapiilani Highway/High Street) and Main Street, just across the street from Kaahumanu Church. Their offices are on the bot-tom floor, and they share them with the Division of Forestry and Wildlife. However, you should address inquiries to each separately. Alas, both are so short-staffed that they will not return calls. The per-son at the counter may know almost nothing about the current state of Maui's trails.

Division of Forestry and Wildlife

At present there are no trails, campgrounds, or cabins under the control of the Division of Forestry and Wildlife for which you are required to have permits for hiking or camping. Surprisingly few of the many areas under this agency's control offer hiking opportunities suitable for the tourist from the mainland. Camping opportunities are almost nil (but see the notes at the ends of Trips E16 and E18). Many areas seem to be managed for hunting but not for hiking. For more information, write or call:

> Department of Land and Natural Resources
> Division of Forestry and Wildlife, Maui District
> P.O. Box 1015
> Wailuku, Maui, HI 96793
> (808) 984-8100
> www.hawaii.gov/dlnr/dfw/dfw.html

See also the note on actually going into Wailuku to see them in person in the paragraph above.

Na Ala Hele

This umbrella organization for a number of groups and agencies has a sensational website at www.hawaiitrails.org. There's lots of good overview information. For individual hikes, not all are covered (not all are under Na Ala Hele's auspices, most notably those in national parks). For those that are covered, the site emphasizes driving directions; maps and hiking directions are minimal.

Let me know what you think and what you find

I hope this book helps make your visit to Maui even more enjoyable than it would have been. I plan to update it regularly, and you can help me. Letters from readers, which I enjoy reading and answering, have been a great help in keeping this book up to date and in planning my repeat visits to Maui. Let me know what you think of this book. Did you find it helpful when you visited Maui? Was it accurate and complete enough that you enjoyed the walks and hikes you took based on the book? Did you notice any significant discrepancies between this book and what you found when you visited Maui, discrepancies that you judge are not just the result of two different perceptions of the same thing? What were they? The publisher and I are very concerned about accuracy. We'd appreciate your comments. I'd also like to know about it if you think there are ways in which the book can be improved. Write to me in care of Wilderness Press, 1200 5th Street, Berkeley, CA 94710, or email: editor@wildernesspress.com.

Spoken Hawaiian:

An Incomplete and Unauthoritative Guide

What, only 12 letters?!

Nineteenth-century American missionaries used only 12 letters to create a written version of the spoken Hawaiian language. Superficially, that might make Hawaiian seem simple. But Hawaiian is a much more complex and subtle language than 12 letters can do justice to. However, we're stuck with those 12 letters, the five English vowels (a, e, i, o, u) and seven of the consonants (h, k, l, m, n, p, w).

Consonants

The consonants have the same sound in Hawaiian as they do in your everyday English except for "w." "W" is sometimes pronounced as "v" when it follows "a," always pronounced as "v" when it follows "e" or "i."

Vowels

The vowels are generally pronounced as they are in Italian, with each vowel sounded separately. Authentic Hawaiian makes further distinctions, but those are of more interest to scholars than to hikers.[1] The following is a simplified system. Vowel sounds in general are:

a   like "ah" in "aha."
e   like "ay" in "day."
i   like "ee" as in "whee!"
o   like "o" in "go."
u   like "oo" in "food" (or "u" in "rude").

Notice that that means that when you see two or more of the same letter in a row, you pronounce each of them separately:

"Kaanapali" is Ka-a-na-pa-li (but everyone pronounces it
        "Ka-na-pa-li").
"Waihee" is Wai-he-e.
"Piilani" is Pi-i-la-ni.
"Hookipa" is Ho-o-ki-pa.
"Puu" is Pu-u.

That seems *too* simple, and it is. If you tried to pronounce every vowel, speaking Hawaiian would turn into a nightmare. You wouldn't live long enough to pronounce some words. Fortunately, several pairs of vowels often—but not always—form merged sounds.

Vowel Pairs Whose Sounds Merge

Like every other language, Hawaiian has vowel pairs whose sounds naturally "smooth" into each other. They're similar to Italian or English diphthongs. The degree to which the two sounds are merged in Hawaiian is officially less than occurs in English, but most Hawaiian

---

1 Remember that Hawaiian evolved as a spoken, not a written, language. Authentic written Hawaiian uses two special marks to indicate other variations on pronouncing vowels in spoken Hawaiian. Those variations change the meaning of a word. One is the glottal stop, indicated by a single quotation mark ('). It indicates that you should make a complete break in your voice before sounding the vowel that follows it. There really isn't an English equivalent, though the break in "uh-oh!" is close. Another is the macron mark, which is a straight line over a vowel. It indicates that you should pronounce a vowel as a long sound instead of a short sound. For example, the Hawaiian long-a sound is "ah," and the Hawaiian short-a sound is "uh." We have the same sounds in English but don't use special marks to distinguish between them except in dictionaries. Road signs, topographic maps, and this book don't use glottal stops or macron marks.

people I've talked with on Kauai merge them fully. Vowel-pair pronunciation is approximately:

ae   often smoothed to "eye" as in "eyeful" or "i" in "ice." It's the English long-i sound.
ai   often smoothed as for "ae," above.
ao   often smoothed to sound like "ow" in "cow."
au   often smoothed to "ow" in "cow", too.
ei   sometimes smoothed to "ay" as in "day." It's the English long-a sound.
eu   smooth the sounds together a *little*, like "ayoo."
oi   usually like "oi" in "oil"—in other words, just what you're used to.

Syllables

Every Hawaiian syllable ends in a vowel sound. A Hawaiian syllable never contains more than one consonant. That means every consonant goes with the vowel that *follows* it. Every vowel *not* preceded by a consonant stands alone when you break a *written* word into syllables (you may smooth some of them together when you *speak*). For example:

"Aa" consists of the two syllables a-a (it's a kind of lava flow).
"Kihei" consists of the three syllables Ki-he-i (but everyone pronounces it "KEE-hay").
"Kipahulu" consists of the four syllables Ki-pa-hu-lu (an area famed for its cascades, falls, and natural swimming pools, now part of Haleakala National Park)
"Haleakala" consists of the five syllables Ha-le-a-ka-la (the dormant volcano that makes up East Maui; the national park that encompasses its upper slopes and a strip of its southeast flank).
"Ulupalakua" consists of the six syllables U-lu-pa-la-ku-a (a huge ranch on the southwest slopes of Haleakala; home of Maui's Tedeschi Winery).
"Liliuokalani" consists of the seven syllables Li-li-u-o-ka-la-ni (Hawaii's last monarch and writer of the beloved song "Aloha Oe").

Accent

In general, the accent falls on the next-to-last syllable for words with three or more syllables and on the first syllable for words of two syllables. For words of more than three syllables, you put a little stress on every other syllable preceding the accented one. Don't worry about this; it seems to come naturally.

There are common-usage exceptions, such as *makai* (ma-KAI, with the accent on the last syllable). When you see exceptions such as those, chances are that what has happened is that European usage has fully merged two sounds into one. Proper Hawaiian pronunciation of *makai* would be closer to "ma-KAH-i," a three-syllable word with the last two syllables almost merging.

Hint for Longer Words: Repetition and Rhythm

Have you noticed the tendency in long Hawaiian words for groups of letters to repeat? That kind of repetition is fairly common. When you see a long Hawaiian word, don't panic. Identify its repeating letter

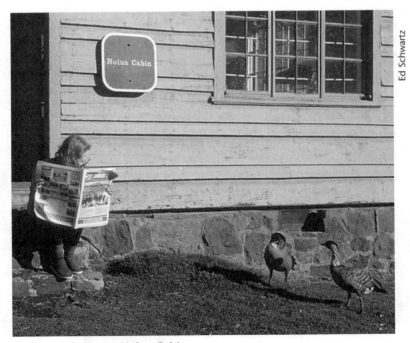

Author and *nene* at Holua Cabin

groups, figure out how to pronounce them individually, then put the whole word together. Chances are you'll come pretty close to getting it correct.

For example, *Waialeale* throws a lot of people. But look at the repeating letter group *ale* (ah-lay). See the word as "Wai/ale/ale." So, two "a-le"s prefixed with a *wai* (the *ai* merges here)—that makes "wai/a-le/a-le." Once you've identified the repeating groups, the rhythm of the word comes naturally. Try this approach for longer words, including the state fish: *humuhumunukunukuapuaa*: two "hu-mu"s, two "nu-ku"s, and an "a-pu-a-a." Now try it: "hu-mu/hu-mu/nu-ku/nu-ku/a-pu-a-a." . . .Very good!

Makai and *mauka*

In Hawaii, local people often give directions or describe the location of a place as *makai* (merge the *ai*), which means "toward the sea," or *mauka* (merge the *au*), which means "toward the mountains; inland." I had a terrible time remembering which was which until I came up with this mnemonic:

> Go *makai*
> Where sea meets sky,

and Tom Winnett came up with:
> *Mauka* is toward the MAUntains.

However, I use the terms left, right, north, south, east, and west. I don't often use *mauka* and *makai* in this book, although I find myself increasingly thinking in those terms!

Do your best, with respect

Approach the language with respect, and give it your best shot. Then be prepared to hear local people pronounce it differently. Learn from them. Maybe it's part of our jobs as visitors to inadvertently provide a little comic relief for those living and working here as opposed to just vacationing here.

Instant Hawaiian (see Bibliography) is a useful booklet that's a lot less frivolous than its title implies. It begins, "So you'd like to learn to speak Hawaiian—you should live so long!" I felt I'd come to the right place. Look for it when you get to Maui.

Geology and History, Natural and Human

First, the earth

According to the theory of *plate tectonics*, the earth consists of:

A rigid, rocky outer shell, the *lithosphere* ("rocky zone")

Beneath the lithosphere, a hot, semifluid layer, the *asthenos-phere* ("weak zone")

A *core* that doesn't play a part in this oversimplified discussion.

The lithosphere is broken into *plates* that move with respect to each other. Hot, fluid material, possibly from the asthenosphere or melted by contact with the asthenosphere, penetrates up through the lithosphere at three kinds of places:

Mid-oceanic ridges, where plates spread apart

Subduction zones, where plates collide and one dives under the other (subducts)

Hot spots, where a plume of molten material appears in the middle of a plate.

Next, the land

It's believed that the Hawaiian Islands exist where the Pacific Plate, on which they ride, is moving northwest across a hot spot. An undersea volcano is built at the place where the plate is over the hot spot. If the volcano gets big enough, it breaks the ocean's surface to become an island. Eventually, the plate's movement carries the island far enough away from the hot spot that volcanism ceases on that island. Erosion, which begins the moment the new island appears above the sea, tears the land down.

The Hawaiian Islands are successively older toward the northwest and younger toward the southeast. Northwestern islands, like Necker, are hardly more than bits of volcanic rock now. Southeastern islands, including the major Hawaiian Islands, are still significant chunks of land. The big island of Hawaii is the youngest and the farthest southeast of the major islands; Maui is the next youngest; and Kauai and Niihau are the oldest and the farthest northwest of the major islands.

The molten material—lava—characteristic of Hawaiian volcanoes is relatively fluid. The fluidity of the lava allows it to spread widely, and repeated eruptions produce broad-based, rounded volcanoes called shield volcanoes. The volcano expels not only flowing lava but also volcanic fragments such as cinder and ash. Alternating layers of these materials build up during periods of volcanic activity.

Erosion has sculpted the exotic landscapes we associate with volcanic tropical islands. Waves pound the volcano's edges, undercutting them and, where the volcano slopes more steeply, forming cliffs. Streams take material from higher on the volcano, cutting valleys into its flanks and depositing the material they carry as alluvium, like the broad alluvial apron formed on the isthmus side of West Maui by the deposits of four of its streams: Waihee, Waiehu, Iao, and Waikapu. New episodes of volcanism wholly or partly fill in those landscapes, and erosional forces immediately begin sculpting the new surface as well as the remaining older surface.

Maui is geologically an infant on an Earth more than four billion years old. Potassium-argon dating of rocks suggests that lava welled forth to build West Maui beginning a little less than two million years ago. Volcanism ended on West Maui just over a million years ago. Haleakala literally burst upon the scene less than a million years ago. Outpourings from Haleakala built the isthmus that now connects West and East Maui. West Maui's volcano, Puu Kukui, may be extinct now; East Maui—Haleakala—is only dormant. The last lava flow on Maui occurred along Haleakala's southwest rift zone in about 1790, forming Cape Kinau and dividing what had been one huge bay into Ahihi and La Pérouse bays. Haleakala may erupt again; no one knows whether it will or when or where. On West Maui, and on East Maui while Haleakala sleeps, erosion reigns, changing the landscape constantly.

Life arrives

Living organisms colonize new land rapidly. In Hawaii, plants established themselves once there was a little soil for them. Seeds arrived on the air currents, too, or floated in from the sea, or hitched a ride on the feathers or in the guts of birds. Insects and spiders also took advantage of the air

Ilima

currents. Birds were certainly among the first visitors. Living things found little competition and quickly adapted to their new home, evolving into an astonishing variety of species many of which occur naturally only on the Hawaiian islands ("endemic to Hawaii"). The only mammals to arrive were the bat and the seal. Some birds became flightless—a fairly common adaptation on isolated islands with no ground predators.

Sandalwood flowers in Hosmer Grove, Haleakala National Park

People arrive

It's unlikely that the site of the very first human colony in the Hawaiian Islands will ever be found. Too much time has passed; too many destructive forces have been at work. However, recent archaeological work has established that people had settled in Hawaii by 300–400 A.D., earlier than had previously been thought. Linguistic studies and cultural artifacts recovered from sites of early colonization point to the Marquesas Islands as the colonizers' home; the Marquesas themselves seem to have been colonized as early as 200 B.C.

The colonizers of Hawaii had to adapt the Marquesan technology to their new home. For example, the Marquesans made distinctive large, one-piece fishhooks from the large, strong pearl shells that abounded in Marquesan waters. There are no such large shells in Hawaiian waters, so the colonists developed two-piece fishhooks made of the weaker materials that were available in Hawaii (such as bone and wood). Over time, a uniquely Hawaiian material culture developed.

At one time, scholars believed that, as related in Hawaii's oral traditions and genealogies, a later wave of colonizers from Tahiti swept in and conquered the earlier Hawaiians. Research does not support that theory. Instead, research has revealed that before European contact, Hawaiian material culture evolved steadily in patterns that suggest gradual and local, not abrupt and external, influences. The archaeological record hints that there may have been some Hawaiian-Tahitian contact in the twelfth century, but its influence was slight.

The Hawaiians profoundly altered the environment of the islands. They had brought with them the plants they had found most useful in the Marquesas Islands: *taro, ti*, the trees from which they made a bark cloth (*kapa*), sugarcane, ginger, gourd plants, yams, bamboo, turmeric, arrowroot, and the breadfruit tree. They also brought the small pigs of Polynesia, dogs, jungle fowl, and, probably as stowaways, rats. They used slash-and-burn technology to clear the native lowland forests for the crops they brought. Habitat loss together with competition for food with and predation by the newly introduced animals wrought havoc with the native animals, particularly birds. Many species of birds had already become extinct long before Europeans arrived.

On the eve of the Europeans' accidentally stumbling across Hawaii, the major Hawaiian islands held substantial numbers of people of Polynesian descent. They had no written language, but their oral and musical traditions were ancient and rich. Their technology apparently remained as static as their rigid social system. Commoners, or *makaainana*, lived in self-sufficient family groups and villages, farming and fishing for most necessities and trading for necessities they could not otherwise obtain. The land was divided among hereditary chiefs of the noble class (*alii*). Commoners paid part of their crops or catches as taxes to the chief who ruled the land-division they lived on; commoners served their chief as soldiers. Higher chiefs ruled over lower chiefs; the higher chiefs received taxes and commoners to serve as soldiers from the lower chiefs in turn. People especially gifted in healing, divination, or important crafts served the populace in those capacities (for example, as priests). There was also a class of untouchables, the *kauwa*. Most people were at death what they were at birth.

Strict laws defined what was forbidden, or *kapu*, and governed the conduct of *kauwa* toward everyone else, of commoners toward *alii*, of *alii* of a lower rank to *alii* of higher rank, and of men and women toward each other. Some of the laws seem irrationally harsh. For example, a commoner could be put to death if his shadow fell on an *alii*.

Chiefs frequently made war on one another. If the chiefs of one island were united under a high chief or a king, often that island would make war on the other islands. In the late 1700s, war raged between Maui and the big island of Hawaii for many years. Hawaii's king was able to hold Maui's Hana district for much of the time, and periodically he tried to conquer the rest of Maui. The young warrior and future king Kamehameha served Hawaii's king and first saw combat in these wars against Maui.

Gods and goddesses

The Hawaiians worshipped many gods and goddesses. The principal ones were Ku, Kane, Kanaloa, and Lono. Ku represented the male aspect of the natural world. Ku was also the god of war, and he demanded human sacrifice. Kane was the god of life, a benevolent god who was regarded as the Creator and the ancestor of all Hawaiians. Kanaloa ruled the dead and the dark aspects of life, and he was often linked with Kane in worship.

Lono was another benevolent god; he ruled clouds, rain, and harvests. The annual winter festival in Lono's honor, Makahiki, ran from October to February. Makahiki was a time of harvest, celebration, fewer *kapu*, and sporting events. Images of Lono were carried around each island atop tall poles with crosspieces from which banners of white tapa flew. (Legend said Lono had sailed away from Hawaii long ago and would return in a floating *heiau* (temple) decked with poles flying long white banners from their crosspieces.) Chiefs and chiefesses met the image of Lono with ceremonies and gifts, and commoners came forward to pay their taxes.

Systems like that can last for hundreds and even thousands of years in the absence of compelling internal problems or changes and of external forces, as the Hawaiian system did. But change eventually comes.

The Europeans arrive by accident

Christopher Columbus had sailed from Spain to what he thought was the Orient, hoping to find a sea route to replace the long, hazardous land route. But in fact he discovered an obstacle called North America. With a direct sea route between Europe and the Orient blocked, people sought other sea routes. The southern routes around the Cape of Good Hope at the tip of Africa and Cape Horn at the tip of South America proved to be very long and very treacherous. Still, the trade was lucrative. The European demand for Oriental goods such as spices, Chinese porcelain, and silk was insatiable. By trading their way around the world, a captain, his crew, and the government or the tradesmen that financed them might become very wealthy in just one voyage.

All over Europe, people came to believe that a good, navigable route *must* exist in northern waters that would allow them to sail west from Europe around the northern end of North America to the Orient. (It doesn't exist.) Captain James Cook sailed from England on July 12, 1776, to try to find the Northwest Passage from the Pacific side.

In December of 1777, Cook left Tahiti sailing northeast, not expecting to see land again until he reached North America. Instead, he sighted land on January 18, 1778, and reached the southeast shore of Kauai on January 19th. In Hawaii, it was the time of *Makahiki*, the festival honoring the god Lono. The Hawaiians mistook the masts and sails of Cook's ships for the poles and *kapa* banners of the floating *heiau* on which Lono was to return. They received Cook as if he were Lono.

Cook was an intelligent and compassionate man who respected the native societies he found and who tried to deal with their people

19

fairly and decently. He tried to keep crewmen who he knew had vene-real diseases from infecting the natives, but he failed. Cook did not stay long in Hawaii. He spent most of 1778 searching for the Northwest Passage; unsuccessful, he returned to Hawaii in early 1779 to make repairs and resupply. It was *Makahiki* again. All went well at first, but the Hawaiians stole an auxiliary boat from one of his ships. When he tried to retrieve it, there was a brief skirmish, in which Cook and four of his crew were killed.

Cook's ships survived a second futile search for the Northwest Passage, after which the crew sailed westward for England, stopping in China. There the crew learned the astonishing value of another of the expedition's great discoveries: the furs of the sea otters and seals of the Pacific Northwest. Trade with the Orient suddenly became even more profitable, and Hawaii was to become not an isolated curiosity but an important point on a major world trade route.

A Young Conquering Chief

In Hawaii, the young chief Kamehameha began his conquest of the islands in 1790. Kamehameha actively sought Western allies, weapons, and advice. He subdued Maui for the first time after a bloody battle in Iao Valley. Maui's defiant king recaptured the island; years passed before Kamehameha reconquered Maui. He conquered all the islands but Kauai and Niihau.

Kamehameha's wars, Western diseases, and the sandalwood trade decimated the native Hawaiians. Chiefs indebted themselves to foreign merchants for weapons and other goods. New England merchants dis-covered that Hawaii had abundant sandalwood for which the Chinese would pay huge prices. Merchants demanded payment in sandalwood. The heartwood nearest the roots was the best part; the whole tree had to be destroyed to get it. The mountains were stripped of their sandal-wood trees. Those ordered into the mountains often died of exposure and starvation. Communities that had depended on their labor for food also starved.

Kamehameha I died in 1819, leaving the monarchy to his son Liholiho and a regency in Liholiho's behalf to his favorite wife, Kaahu-manu. Liholiho was an amiable, weak-willed alcoholic. Kaahumanu was strong-willed, intelligent, capable, and ambitious. She believed that the old Hawaiian *kapu* system was obsolete: no gods struck down the Westerners, who daily did things that were *kapu* for Hawaiians. Six

Kaupo

months after Kamehameha I's death, she persuaded Liholiho to join her in breaking several ancient *kapu*. The *kapu* system, discredited, crumbled; the old order was dead.

The missionaries arrive

Congregationalist missionaries from New England reached Hawaii in 1820; Liholiho grudgingly gave them a year's trial. The end of the *kapu* system had left a religious vacuum into which the missionaries moved remarkably easily. To their credit, they came with a sincere desire to commit their lives to bettering those of the people of Hawaii. Liholiho's mother converted to Christianity and made it acceptable for other alii to follow her example. Kaahumanu became a convert, too, and set about remodeling Hawaii socially and politically, based on the Ten Commandments.

An ecosystem passes

Cook and those who came after him gave cattle, goats, and large European pigs as gifts to the Hawaiian chiefs, and the animals overran the islands. They ate everything. Rainwater sluiced off the now-bare hillsides without replenishing the aquifers. Areas that had been blessed with an abundance of water suffered drought now. Native plants could not reestablish themselves because the unrestrained animals ate them as soon as they sent up a shoot. People wrongly concluded that native plants were inherently unable to reestablish themselves, and they imported non-native trees like the eucalyptuses and ironwoods that you see so often today.

The native habitat area and diversity shrank still more before the new sugar plantations. Planters drained wetlands for the commercially valuable crop and erected dams, ditches, and sluices to divert the natural water supply into a controllable water supply. What they did was not so very different from what the Polynesians had done when they had cleared the native lowland forests in order to plant their taro, but the scale was far vaster. In one particularly terrible mistake, growers imported the mongoose to prey on the rats that damaged their crops. But the rat forages at night, while the mongoose hunts by day: they seldom met. What the mongooses preyed on instead were the eggs of native ground-nesting birds.

Few of Hawaii's native plants put forth showy flowers or set palatable fruit, so the new settlers imported ornamental and fruiting plants to brighten their gardens and tables. Many shrubs and trees did so well in Hawaii's favorable climate that they escaped into the wild to become pest plants, crowding out native species and interrupting the food chain.

Birds brought over as pets escaped to compete with native species. More species of native birds have become extinct in Hawaii than anywhere else in the world, and most of the birds you see will be introduced species like the zebra dove and the myna.

It is tragic but true that when you visit Hawaii, you will probably see very few of its native plants and animals. The dryland forest on Haleakala's upper, western slopes and the alpine plants in Haleakala's crater, now fenced to keep out goats and pigs, offer you chances to see remnants of native Hawaiian plant communities.

A culture passes

Literacy replaced the rich Hawaiian oral tradition, and many legends and stories were forgotten before someone thought to write them down. The significance of many place names, apart from their literal meaning, has been lost forever. Zealous missionaries and converts believed that the native traditions were evil, and they nearly succeeded in eradicating all traces of the native culture.

A nation passes

Hawaiians saw that their only hope of surviving as an independent nation in the modern world was to secure the protection and guarantees of freedom of one of the major powers. The Hawaiian monarchs would have preferred the British, but British influence was ultimately inadequate to withstand American influence. American missionaries doled out God's grace. American entrepreneurs established plantations and businesses. American ships filled the harbors. Economic and cultural domination of Hawaii eventually passed into American hands, particularly after the new land laws of 1850 made it possible for foreigners to own land in Hawaii. The Hawaiian monarchy lasted until 1893, but most of its economic and therefore its political power was gone. Hawaii as an independent nation disappeared soon after.

Maui Historical Society Museum

The Maui Historical Society Museum is well worth a visit. It's in Hale Hoikeike, formerly known as Bailey House, at 2375-A Main Street, Wailuku, Maui, HI 96793, telephone (808) 244-3326. Call to check on its hours. You can easily include a visit to the museum as part of your day of seeing Kepaniwai County Park and Iao Valley State Park (see Trips W5 through W7). The house itself dates from the missionary era and is home to a good bookstore/gift shop and to exhibits of Hawaiian craftsmanship and missionary life. Missionary Edward Bailey, who lived here with his family for 45 years beginning in 1840, was also an artist whose works, on display here, record many scenes of nineteenth-century Maui life. A preserved oo in one of the exhibit cases offers the only chance you and I are likely to get to see that probably-now-extinct native bird. The museum asks for a modest donation.

A race passes

The native Hawaiian people lost much of their importance in the changing, Westernized economy early in the nineteenth century. The burgeoning sugar and pineapple plantations needed laborers, and the Hawaiians were diligent, capable hired hands when they wanted to be. But they did not comprehend the idea of hiring themselves out as day laborers for wages. Planters began to import laborers from other parts of the world: China, Japan, the Philippines, Portugal. Many imported laborers stayed, married, raised families, and went on to establish their own successful businesses. The Hawaiians were soon a minority in their own land.

The numbers of full-blooded Hawaiians declined precipitously throughout the nineteenth century. Beginning with the tragic introduction of venereal disease by Cook's men, venereal diseases swept through the native population who, particularly at Makahiki, exchanged partners freely. Venereal disease often leaves its victims sterile, and many who had survived Western diseases, wars, and the sandalwood trade were unable to reproduce. Others married foreigners, so their children were only part Hawaiian. Today most authorities believe that there are no full-blooded Hawaiians left, not even on Niihau, the only island where Hawaiian is still the language of everyday life.

Hawaii becomes American

In the late nineteenth century, the Hawaiian monarchy seemed to some powerful businessmen and civic leaders of American descent to get in the way of the smooth conduct of business. They thought Hawaii would be better off as an American territory. Queen Liliuokalani did not agree. She wanted to assert Hawaii's independence and the authority of its monarchs. The business community plotted a coup, deposed Liliuokalani in 1893, formed a new government, and petitioned the United States for territorial status. The United States formally annexed Hawaii in 1898.

Military projects and mass travel brought mainland Americans flooding into Hawaii. Many stayed, and so the majority of people in Hawaii came to see themselves as Americans, though a minority disagreed (some still do). After many years as a territory, Hawaii became the fiftieth state in 1959.

Things to come

The huge tourist industry is both a blessing and a curse. Massive development pushes the Hawaii-born off the land to make way for hotels. Displaced Hawaiians, whatever their ethnic background, find themselves having to survive as waiters, chambermaids, clerks—in essence, as the servants of those who have displaced them. Many also fear that tourism will result in the Hawaiian paradise being paved over and lost forever; others feel that it already has been. The story of Hawaii's evolution is far from over.

Highways, Transportation, and Trail Maps

Driving

Maui has no public transportation. That leaves most of us dependent on a car, which you should arrange for well in advance of your visit. Ask for a modest vehicle in a drab color so it's inconspicuous when parked at trailheads. Get a road map of Maui in advance, perhaps from one of the national automobile clubs if you belong to one. Even better, get the excellent "Map of Maui" published by the University of Hawaii Press. It's good to be able to study the map in advance and have some notion of the island's roads before you tackle them. Some of the maps provided by tourist bureaus are so cute they're useless.

Driving conditions on Maui vary widely, and driving time can make serious inroads on your hiking time. Major roads between Wailuku and Kahului and Pukalani, Lahaina, and Kihei have stretches where the legal limit is 55 mph. However, look out for traffic jams around Lahaina, Wailuku, Kahului (particularly near the airport), and Kihei. Road construction and the periodic burning of canefields can slow traffic and even close roads. And some roads, described below, are in a class of their own.

Hana and Kipahulu

The road to Hana (Hana Highway—Highway 36, then Highway 360) has been improved to the point where everyone can take surviving the road to Hana for granted. The entire road is paved to and through Hana. The first 16 miles from Kahului and through Paia are rather easy. After it becomes Highway 360, however, it's extremely slow (10 mph recommended), winding, and narrow (often just one lane wide, where drivers going one way may have to stop for traffic going the other way). The Hana Highway is not a seacoast drive, despite its coastal location. It's a rainforest drive; one writer aptly described it as "burrowing through a tunnel of green." It may also be jammed with sightseers. The road becomes Highway 31 after Hana.

Kipahulu to Kaupo

Highway 31 gets worse beyond the Kipahulu District of Haleakala National Park, though it is currently paved at least as far as Alelele Stream except for one 3-mile stretch. However, it is so narrow and winding that signs are posted warning you to sound your horn before going around a curve. It eventually degenerates into a twisting, un-paved 4WD road with oil-pan-eating rocks (we did not make it to Kaupo from the Hana side). This stretch is subject to storm damage. To get to Kaupo, it's better to drive there from the west, through Keokea and Ulupalakua.

Kaupo to Ulupalakua

The road is less winding near Kaupo, but some stretches are cov-ered with smooth beach pebbles offering poor traction. The pavement resumes for good several miles west of Kaupo, but the road remains narrow and slow until Ulupalakua (15 mph recommended). Have a full gas tank if you drive to Kaupo, as there's no gas east of Keokea and west of Hana. The Kaupo Store is open and keeping regular hours, so you can get drinks and snacks there (see Trip E14 for details).

Around the north end of West Maui

The road around the north end of West Maui (Highway 30 north of Kapalua; Highway 340 north of Wailuku) is slow, narrow, winding, and not particularly scenic. I can't recommend it between the turnoff to Waihee Ridge (Trip W1) and Nakalele Blowhole (Trip W12).

Polipoli

The 10-mile road from Highway 377 to Polipoli is narrow, steep, winding, and very slow. Its last 4 miles are unpaved and vary from deep dust to protruding rocks to lumpy clay. Allow at least an hour each way just for this road, if it is passable at all. It it's not passable, park on the shoulder near the end of the paved part and make an enjoyable hike out of the unpaved part (about 6½ miles, total, with negligible elevation changes until you drop down into Polipoli State Park).

What to leave in the car

Nothing. Never leave valuables in your car, even in a locked trunk. "Valuables" include not only jewelry, money, checks, and credit cards but things you can't readily replace: glasses, prescription medication, identification, keys, snapshots of loved ones, etc. Maui may seem a paradise, but there are still a few snakes in the grass.

Hiking

Road maps are useless for hiking trails. For trail maps, I recommend the maps in this book and the United States Geological Survey (USGS) 7½' series of topographic ("topo") maps for Maui. Topos show elevation details as well as roads and trails. However, topos are not updated as often as you'd like. That's why you should use them in conjunction with the maps in this book and information from the agencies in charge of the island's hiking areas—the Division of State Parks, Maui District, and the Division of Forestry and Wildlife, Maui District. If you do not write for these in advance, you will need to go into Wailuku to get them. See their addresses in "Getting Permits or Permission" in this book.

Those visiting Haleakala National Park will appreciate Earthwalk Press's Haleakala National Park Recreation Map. The map includes topographic data, trail descriptions, and a wealth of other information. If you can't find their maps in your travel store, call them at (800) 828-MAPS.

Maui is covered by 17 topos, as shown in the illustration on the next page. It's also nice to have the USGS Maui County topo map. If your mainland backpacking store does not carry the Maui topos, you can get them from: www.usgs.gov

Follow the links to the current site for sales of published products.

USGS 7½ Topographic Maps of Maui

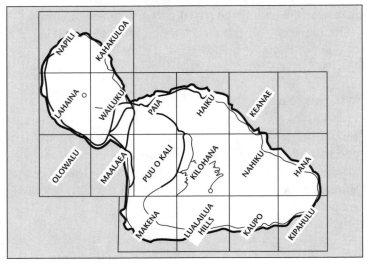

Weather

The short of it

Maui's eastern and western lobes are almost like two separate islands. Each is:

- Rainier on its north side, which boasts rainforests. Waihee Valley on West Maui is a rainforest. The Hana Highway on East Maui tunnels through a rainforest.
- Less rainy on its east side, but still rainy enough to support lush tropical growth. Iao Valley State Park on West Maui is filled with dense tropical vegetation. Hana on the east end of East Maui is famous for its frequent rain, hothouse climate, and colorful gardens.
- Driest and hottest on the south and west. These areas lie in the rain shadow of the volcano that dominates the lobe. Lahaina on the west side of West Maui averages only 17 inches of rain annually and can be fiery hot. Kihei, Wailea, and Makena lie in Haleakala's rain shadow and are not only hot and dry but also frequently very windy, especially in the afternoon.
- Rainy in the mountains, especially between 5000 and 7000 feet.

The isthmus is generally dry and windy. The south and west coasts attract the most visitors, are where the resorts are located, and have the most popular beaches. The figure at the top of the next page summarizes the situation.

The long of it

Hawaii's weather is temperate to a degree that puts the so-called "temperate" zones of the world to shame. The humidity is moderate, too: 50 to 60%, not the sweltering horror of some other tropical lands. It is warmer in the summer and cooler in the winter, but the extremes are nothing like on the mainland.

Hawaii's mild climate is determined largely by its tropical location and also by the northeast trade winds that sweep across it. The northeast trade winds—so-called because sea captains took advantage of them on their trade routes—are dependable, steady winds that blow from the northeast across the thousands of miles of open sea that separate the Hawaiian Islands from the continents. They are responsible for keeping the temperature and the humidity moderate. Since they are the prevailing winds in this area, the side of the island that faces them is called the "windward" side. The opposite side of the island is the opposite of windward; in nautical terms, "leeward."

Sometimes the trade winds fail and are replaced by "kona" winds coming from the south. "Kona" means "leeward," because it's the leeward side of the island that more or less faces these occasional winds. Kona winds bring hot, sticky air. Fortunately, they are rare in summer, when they would be really unpleasant, and occur mostly in winter, when the lower overall temperatures moderate their effect. Kona storms are subtropical low-pressure systems that occur in winter, move in from the south, and can cause serious damage. There is apparently no pattern to them; in some years, they do not occur at all, but in others they occur every few weeks.

Maui Weather Map

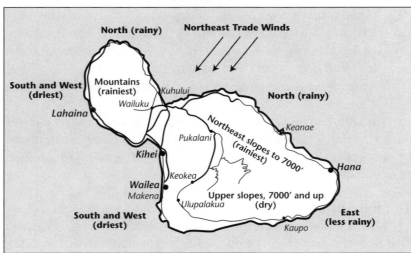

On Maui, average temperatures along the coast range from highs of 79–87° F to lows of 62–70° F. The "cooler" ones are winter temperatures, the warmer ones summer. It's rainier from November through March than it is the rest of the year. Expect cooler temperatures, more wind, and considerably more rain if you are in a mountainous region (my thermometer read 40° F one clear morning in Haleakala crater).

Nanea (top) and beach *naupaka* (below)

Equipment Suggestions and Miscellaneous Hints

This book isn't intended to teach you *how* to hike or backpack. If you can walk, you can hike, especially the "very easy" hikes. You can learn about backpacking in *Backpacking Basics* by Thomas Winnett and Melanie Findling (see Bibliography). Just be sure the trip you pick is within *your* hiking limits.

This book is intended specifically to let you know where you can hike on Maui, what to expect when you hike there, and how to get to the trailhead for each hike. And that, I hope, will help you decide *which* hikes to take.

This section will give you information to help you plan a successful trip and suggestions to make your hikes even more pleasant, and perhaps better protect you and the environment. Of course, you're the only person who lives in your body, so you'll have to judge what's really appropriate for you. But there are a few things you might want to know before you go—things that may be very different from the hiking you've done at home on the mainland. (Maybe you already know them, but it's hard to shut me up when I think I have some good advice.)

32

It's up to you

No book can substitute for, or give you, five things only you can supply: physical fitness, preparedness, experience, caution, and common sense. Don't leave the trailhead without them.

What to take

Minimum equipment for strolls and easy dayhikes

You don't need to make extensive preparations for a stroll along a beach or a half-mile nature trail as long as there's food, water, and shelter nearby— perhaps in your car. The things you must not go without are:

- Sunglasses
- Appropriate footwear
- Strong sunblock applied *before* you set out
- Mosquito repellent (jungle juice)

DEET

Your mosquito repellent should be "jungle juice"—that is, have a high percentage of DEET (diethyltoluamide). DEET is pretty vile stuff, but it works.

Minimum equipment for moderate and strenuous hikes

Carry at least the Ten Essentials Plus One as I've adapted them from the Sierra Club. Besides sturdy boots, they are:

Pack (to put these good things in; could be a large fanny pack)

Food and water (assume that all open water sources are unsafe to drink)

Extra clothing (always take rain gear, as it can rain any time on Maui)

Map (and compass if you can use it)

Flashlight with extra bulbs and batteries

Sunglasses and strong sunblock applied before you set out

Means to dig a hole 6–8 inches deep and at least 200 feet from water, in order to bury solid body wastes; tissue that you will also bury (or pack out)

Pocket knife

First-aid kit

33

Waterproof matches and something you can keep a flame going with
(such as a candle) only when necessary to start a fire in order to
save a life

Mosquito repellent ("jungle juice" as described above)

Equipment for backpacks

The following is a minimal checklist for backpacking equipment.

Backpack	Tent	Sleeping pad
Sleeping bag	Permit	
Ten Essentials Plus One (above)		
Boots	Socks	Shirts
Shorts or long pants	Hat	Rain gear
Underwear	Toiletries	Personal medication
Stove and fuel*	Eating utensils	
Cookware and clean-up stuff		

* You cannot take stove fuel on a plane. You must buy it at your destination. Be sure
your stove's fuel tank and any fuel bottles you take are empty before you pack them.

Shoes

Tennis shoes?

I've noted in the hike descriptions whether tennis shoes are okay
to wear or whether I think you should wear boots. I base that recom-
mendation on the length of the hike and the difficulty of the terrain.
What tennis shoes may lack that boots can provide are ankle support
and soles that grip. Only you can really decide how important those
are to you.

Boots

If you're going to hike a lot, be sure your boot seams are freshly
sealed and you've freshly waterproofed the entire boot, including the
cloth part, if any. Use a heavy-duty waterproofing compound like a
wax, and bring some of it along in order to renew the coating if necessary. Chances are your boots will get wet, especially in the winter. And
they'll stay wet, because things dry slowly in the tropical humidity. It's
pretty tough on the boots and, together with the abrasion of mud particles, could cause boot seams to fail.

Hiking stick

Take your hiking stick if you usually hike with one. The flight attendants can put it in the closet where they hang the carry-on suits and dresses or in the overhead compartments. Maui's terrain can be very slippery when wet, and a hiking stick can be a big help in maintaining your footing. And it can double as a spider stick (see below).

Spider stick

There are a very few overgrown trails where you and some orb spiders may meet unexpectedly, head-on. You probably don't like collecting spiders with your face, but these critters make it hard not to do so. Here's one way to avoid them without killing them. Pick up and use a "spider stick"—a long, strong stick that you carefully wave up and down in front of you as you hike through brushy country. You can feel the tug when the stick connects with a web. Detach the anchor strands that hold the web in your way, and lay them aside on the adjacent shrubbery. An orb spider normally rebuilds most or all of its web daily, so you've caused it only minor inconvenience. Your hiking stick can probably double as a spider stick.

Sleeping bag

It should be able to tolerate wet conditions. For example, it could have a Gore-Tex shell or it could have a synthetic fill. You are almost certain to get rained on a bit while camping.

Tent

You'll need one for protection from the rain.

Clothes while backpacking

On the one hand, it's best to go as light as possible; on the other hand, almost nothing—not even synthetics—dries overnight in Maui's damp climate under backpacking conditions. Consider which things you can stand to wear damp and which you can't stand unless they're dry. Pack just one or two of the "okay if damp" things. Pack a set of the "gotta be dry!" things for each day plus one or more extras, just in case. (For me, it's socks.)

At the end of a soggy day of camping out

On those occasional rainy days, you may wonder how you're going to get reasonably clean without getting any wetter than you already are. The socks you've worn all day are "goners" for the time being, wet and muddy on the outside but relatively clean on the inside. While you're changing into dry clothes, turn your "used" socks inside out and mop yourself off with them.

Getting hiking and backpacking food

If you are planning to backpack on Maui, consider shopping for your hiking and backpacking chow on Maui. Food prices are higher in Hawaii, but you have enough stuff to put in your luggage without bringing your food, too. There are several well-stocked supermarkets on the island, particularly around Kahului, Kihei, and Lahaina. I couldn't find freeze-dried chow, but there was an adequate selection of long-lasting, lightweight, quick-cooking foods.

Cautions and Hazards

Hypothermia? On Maui?

It's possible if you go into the mountains. Remember that going higher is equivalent to going north into colder climates, and mountains are often very windy. Please be prepared as you would be for going into any mountainous region.

Biodegradable? Ha, ha, ha!

The following things are popularly supposed to be biodegradable if you bury them: toilet tissue; facial tissue; sanitary napkins; tampons; disposable diapers. That must be a joke. They often last long enough for either running water to exhume them or animals to dig them up. It's actually pretty easy to carry them out if you put them in a heavy-duty self-sealing bag. I use a quart-size Ziploc bag. If I'm feeling squeamish about handling an item, I'll coax it into the bag with the help of a small stick.

Pest plants

As I mentioned in the chapter on geology and history, introduced plants have overrun Hawaii. It's important to try to control the spread of these plants. One thing you can do to help is to wash the soil, and with it the seeds of any pest plants, you hope, off of your shoes or boots before you leave a hiking area. Note also that you, like any other animal, can carry pest-plant seeds in your digestive tract and deposit them, ready to sprout, in your solid wastes. Either hold it till you get to a toilet or dig your hole deep enough to make it impossible for the seeds to sprout (one foot deep, according to a pamphlet on the subject. I have no idea how to dig a hole one-foot deep with a shovel that hikers can reasonable carry; I'm just telling you what I've read). Pest plants include all the guavas. For more information, call the Hawaii State Department of Agriculture, (808) 548-7119, Weed Control Section.

Companions

The standard advice is: never hike alone; never camp alone.

Water

Take your own drinking water for the day. Plan on treating water while backpacking. No open source of water anywhere in the U.S. is safe to drink untreated. Treat water chemically (iodine or chlorine preparations designed for the purpose) or by boiling (1–5 minutes at a rolling boil). It now seems that filtering may be ineffective against the bacterium that causes leptospirosis (below). Backpacking opportunities on Maui are, in my opinion, limited to Haleakala crater where the drinking water supply is rain collected from the roofs of the cabins and stored in closed tanks, so that it is presumed to be safe to drink. Tap water at these campgrounds is reported to be safe to drink: Hosmer Grove Campground; Polipoli State Park; and Waianapanapa State Park. There is no safe drinking water at Kipahulu; you must treat stream water there (or, better yet, fill your jugs with clean water at Hana).

Avoiding leptospirosis

Fresh water on Maui may be contaminated with the bacterium that causes leptospirosis. A pamphlet about leptospirosis is available from the Epidemiology Branch of the Hawaii State Department of Health (on Maui, call (808) 244-4288). The following summarizes some of its contents: Muddy and clear water are both suspect. The bacterium invades through broken skin or the nose, mouth, or eyes. It enters the bloodstream and infects different organs, particularly the kidneys. Precautions that would especially apply to you here are not to go into streams if you have open cuts or abrasions and not to drink (untreated) stream water. Treat water chemically or by boiling it.

If you do swim in fresh water on Maui, you should know that the incubation period of leptospirosis is 2–20 days. The onset is sudden, and the symptoms may resemble those of flu: fever, chills, sweating, severe headache, conjunctivitis (red eyes), muscle pains, weakness, vomiting, and diarrhea. You should see a physician immediately if you suspect leptospirosis. It's believed that administering certain antibiotics early in the course of the disease will shorten the disease and make symptoms less severe. The pamphlet says that most cases are mild and that people (with mild cases) recover in a week or two without treatment. However, severe leptospirosis infections may damage kidneys, liver, or heart or even cause death.

Sun

I can't overemphasize the importance of protecting your skin from the sun. Not only is skin cancer a serious, potentially fatal problem, but a sunburn will ruin at least part of your vacation—maybe even keep you off the trail for a few days (gadzooks!). Sun exposure also ages your skin. Americans are realizing that a "glorious tan" today means wrinkled, leathery skin and skin cancer tomorrow. Sun protection is especially important at higher altitudes where the amount of ultraviolet radiation (the cancer-causing rays) striking your skin is much greater than at sea level.

Short of staying indoors, your major lines of defense are clothing and sunblock. Instead of T-shirts and tank-tops, wear lightweight but opaque, long-sleeved shirts. Consider wearing long pants instead of shorts. Wear a hat with a brim sufficient to shade your face. Lightweight gloves will protect hands, which always seem to get burnt no matter how much sunblock you put on them.

For sunblock, choose the highest "sun protection factor" (SPF) number of water-resistant cream or lotion you can find from a reputable manufacturer. Spray-on products are less effective. Apply as directed to face, ears, neck, and any other areas that may be exposed. Allow 20–30 minutes for the sunblock to react with your skin to form a protective barrier. Reapply as necessary. Don't forget to use a sun-blocking lip-protectant, too.

When using sunblock with insect repellent, apply the sunblock first and give it time to "bond" with your skin before applying the repellent. The only effective repellent, DEET, reduces the effectiveness of sunblock, so this is another reason to get the highest SPF sunblock you can find. Don't waste your money on products that combine sunblock and insect repellent; they're self-defeating.

And don't imagine that lots of natural skin pigmentation will protect you. The worst sunburn I ever saw was on a friend of mine who thought that because she was black, she didn't need sunblock. Personally, I use an SPF 50, water-resistant, baby-formula, unscented sunblock with titanium dioxide every day, rain or shine, indoors or out, and carry more in the car. That way, I'm set to go when the urge to hike hits.

Using This Book

How This Book Organizes the Trips

Imagine the hour hand of a clock pinned to a point near the center of a rounded island. Think of it sweeping around clockwise from a 12-o'clock position that's due north. It's easy to envision the hour hand pointing to 3 o'clock (due east), 6 o'clock (due south), and 9 o'clock (due west) as it moves around.

You can think of Maui, with its two rounded lobes, as two clocks, one for the west lobe and another for the east lobe. I've added a third clock just for Haleakala.

The West Maui "clock"

The West Maui "clock" has its hour hand pivoted on Puu Kukui, its highest point, and its hour hand sweeps clockwise around West Maui. For convenience's sake, I'll consider the isthmus to be part of the West Maui clock. Trips on West Maui and the isthmus start at the 2-o'clock point with Waihee Ridge (Trip W1). Here's the West Maui clock at right:

The East Maui "clock"

The East Maui "clock" has its hour hand pivoted on a point that's about halfway up the highway to Haleakala. Trips on East Maui start near 1 o'clock at Waikamoi Ridge (Trip E1). Distances are much more compressed on the East Maui clock than they are on the West Maui clock: East Maui is much larger than West Maui, but both "clocks" need to fit into the same space for this book. Here's the East Maui clock at right:

The Haleakala "clock"

Distances are so compressed on the East Maui clock that it would be very hard to use it to show the hikes that start in and around Haleakala's crater. Yet that's the most important single hiking area on Maui! Hikes in that area are all together at the end of the book and have their own "clock" that's an enlargement of the East Maui clock area around Haleakala's crater.

They are numbered H1, H2, etc., beginning with the Hosmer Grove Nature Loop (Trip H1) a little past 3 o'clock.

How to Read the Trip Descriptions

The trip descriptions are in the following format, and here is what the information in each description means:

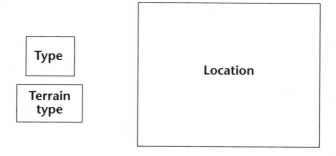

Distance	Elevation gain	Hiking time	Topos
4¼ miles	370'	2+ hours	*Wailuku 7½'*

Difficulty: *Moderate, hiking boots strongly recommended.*

Highlights: *This may be the best of the rainforest stream-valley walks on Maui.*

Title (pretty self-explanatory).

Type

There are four types of trips described:

Loop trips: You follow trails that form a closed loop; you don't retrace your steps, or you retrace them for only a proportionally short distance.

Semiloop trips: The trip consists of a loop portion and an out-and-back portion.

Out-and-back trips: This is by far the most common type of trip in this book. You follow trails to a specified destination and then retrace your steps to your starting point.

Shuttle trips: You start at one trailhead and finish at another, "destination" trailhead. They are far enough apart (or walking between them is sufficiently impractical) that you need to have a car waiting for you at your "destination" trailhead or to have someone pick you up there.

Terrain type

Icons give you a general idea of the kind of terrain you'll be walking. Some hikes offer mixed terrain; for them, I've tried to indicate the terrain type where you'll spend the most walking time:

 Inland; hilly or mountainous

 Near or at the ocean, such as along a beach or on cliffs above the sea

Location

The inset map illustrates the trip's general location relative to the rest of Maui.

Distance: The distance is the total distance you have to walk.

Elevation Gain: This figure is the approximate net elevation change between the hike's highest and lowest points.

Hiking time: This is based on my normal hiking speed, which is a blazing 2 miles/hour.

Topos: The topo or topos listed here are the ones that cover the area you'll be hiking in on this particular trip. As all the listed topos are 7½′ topos, I shan't bother to repeat "7½′" for each listing. Topos are strictly optional for the very easy and easy trips but are strongly recommended for the other trips.

Trail map

Only listed if the map cannot be found near the "Description." See the end of this chapter for the trail map conventions.

Difficulty and suggested shoes

A trip's difficulty is based first on total distance and second on cumulative elevation gain and rate of gain. Let's say that the elevation gain is negligible to moderate (it's never steeper than about 500 feet/mile for any significant distance). In that case:

A **very easy** trip is 1 mile or less.

An **easy** trip is more than 1 mile but not more than 2 miles.

A **moderate** trip is more than 2 miles but not more than 5 miles.

A **strenuous** trip is more than 5 miles.

If the trip has a section of, say, a half-mile or more where it's steeper than 500 feet/mile, or if the trail is hard to follow, then I've given it the next higher difficulty rating.

Some trips just aren't safe if you're not wearing boots with soles that grip and which will give you some ankle support. However, only *you* live in your body, so you will have to be the final judge of what you can safely wear. Bare feet are never safe, in my opinion, except perhaps on a less-used beach. The standard wording follows:

Tennis shoes recommended

Hiking boots strongly recommended

Hiking boots mandatory—the route is very rough.

Highlights

This gives you an idea of what I think the best features of the trip are. Usually, it's the scenery—that's one of the principal things you came to Maui for!

Driving instructions: This gives you instructions for driving to the trailhead, usually in terms of driving from Lihue. You may be staying anywhere on Kauai, but Lihue is a convenient reference point. Be sure you have a good road map of Kauai to supplement these instructions.

Permits/permission required: A few trips require you to have someone's permission to camp. This section will tell you what you need permission for, if anything, and whom to apply to. See "Permits" for addresses.

Description: This gives you instructions for driving to the trailhead, usually in terms of driving from Wailuku, the county seat. You may be staying anywhere on Maui, but Wailuku is a convenient reference point. The starting point in Wailuku is the intersection of Highways 30 and 32 (High Street and Main Street, respectively). Kaahumanu Church and the State Office Building are on the south corners of that intersection, and you must go through that intersection on your way to what's likely to be your first sightseeing destination, Iao Valley State Park.

Some trips simply aren't feasible unless you're staying much nearer to them than Wailuku. Trips like that include those in the Hana area (I recommend you stay in Hana), the Kipahulu District (again, stay in Hana), Polipoli (stay in Polipoli), and Haleakala crater (backpack into the crater). Those trips are treated as side trips from the nearest place where it's practical for you to stay.

Be sure you have a good road map of Maui to supplement these instructions.

Supplemental information

At the bottom of most of the trips, there's some extra information about the historical significance of places you'll see along the route. Or maybe there's a story—a myth, for example—related to the trip which I hope will add to your enjoyment of the trip. Perhaps there'll be a bit more information about the plants or the geology in the area. I put most of the supplemental information at the end so that it wouldn't interfere too much with the description of the trip itself. I think safety dictates that you give your attention first to the trip and only secondarily to the supplemental information. (That is not a problem with very easy hikes, so the supplemental information is often part of the main description in those hikes.)

Icon Key

Geologic or Hydrologic
Feature

General Information

Local History

Hawaiian Traditions and
Legends

Animals/Birds

Botanical Feature

Side Trip

45

Map Legend

Keanae Pt.

Moku Holua

Old Keanae Landing

KEANAE HOMESTEADS

Keanae

Keanae Uka △ **T**
Start/end Trip E2

360

N

Piinaau Stream

Palauhulu Stream

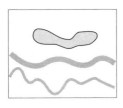

Land

Body of water, ocean

River, large stream

Stream

0	1/4	1/2	1 mile

 =56= =560= Highway

———————— Paved road

= = = = = Unpaved road

River Name   Self-explanatory

Stream Name   Self-explanatory

T Trip 1   Trailhead for number‹ trip(s)

– – – – – –   Trail

. . . .   Use trail or route whe‹ there is no trail as suc‹ (e.g., along a beach)

ROCK TRAIL   Trail name (if any)

★   Destination of trip

★ **Trip 1**   Destination of trip or‹ trail with more than one destination

Keanae Uka △
402   Named benchmark w‹ elevation

† or Cem   Cemetery

2261 Papau x   Named point and elevation

KEANAE HOMESTEADS   Additional named topo feature

▲   Campground

▲   Cabin

♦   Headquarters

⊼   Picnic tables

∿   Truncation (item cut short—doesn't apply)

/   Gate

⸸   Lighthouse

Hiking Table

The following hiking table summarizes all the trips in this book. It will help you quickly decide which trips interest you and which are within your party's abilities.

The following abbreviations are used in the hiking table: **b'pk** is backpack; **O&B** is an out-and-back hike.

Trip Number and Name	Best As...	Type	Difficulty	Miles
West Maui Hikes				
W1. Waihee Ridge	Dayhike	O&B	Moderate	4½
W2. Waihee Valley	Dayhike	O&B	Moderate	4¼
W3. Halekii-Pihana	Dayhike	O&B	Very easy	⅖
W4. Kahana Pond	Dayhike	O&B	Very easy	—
W5. Kepaniwai Park	Dayhike	Loop	Very easy	2/3
W6. Iao Nature Trail	Dayhike	Semiloop	Very easy	¼
W7. Iao Needle/Streamside	Dayhike	O&B	Easy	1½
W8. Maalaea Beach	Dayhike	O&B	Moderate	4
W9. Lahaina Pali Trail	Dayhike	Shuttle	Strenuous	5
W10. Olowalu: Petroglyph	Dayhike	O&B	Easy	1
W11. D.T. Fleming	Dayhike	Semiloop	Easy	1¾
W12. Nakalele Blowhole	Dayhike	O&B	Easy	1
East Maui Hikes				
E1. Waikamoi Ridge	Dayhike	Semiloop	Easy	⅓-1⅛
E2. Arboretum	Dayhike	O&B	Easy	1
E3. Puaa Kaa	Dayhike	O&B	Very easy	—
E4. Ulaino Road	Dayhike	O&B	Moderate	4
E5. Caves	Dayhike	O&B	Very easy	⅕
E6. Black Sand Beach	Dayhike	O&B	Very easy	¹⁄₁₀
E7. King's Hwy-North	Dayhike	O&B	Strenuous	2⅔

E8. King's Hwy-*Heiau*	Dayhike	O&B	Easy	1½
E9. King's Hwy-Bay	Dayhike	O&B	Strenuous	5
E10. Hana Bay	Dayhike	O&B	Very easy	½
E11. Oheo Gulch/Pools	Dayhike	Loop	Very easy	⅔
E12. Makahiku Falls	Dayhike	O&B	Easy	⅔
E13. Waimoku Falls	Dayhike	O&B	Moderate	4
E14. Kaupo to Boundary	Dayhike	O&B	Strenuous	6½
E15. Waihou Spring Trail	Dayhike	Semiloop	Moderate	3
E16. Ranger's Cabin	Dayhike	O&B	Moderate	3
E17. Kahua Road	Dayhike	O&B	Strenuous	9
E18. Skyline Trail	Dayhike	O&B	Strenuous	13
E19. King's Hwy-Kanaio	Dayhike	O&B	Moderate	4
E20. Puu Olai	Dayhike	Semiloop	Moderate	1½
E21. Polo Beach	Dayhike	O&B	Very easy	⅔
E22. Kamaole Beach	Dayhike	O&B	Very easy	1

Haleakala Hikes

H1. Hosmer Grove	Dayhike	Loop	Very easy	⅔
H2. Supply Trail	Dayhike	O&B	Strenuous	5⅓
H3. Halemauu-View	Dayhike	O&B	Easy	1½
H4. Halemauu-Holua	Dayhike	O&B	Strenuous	8
	2-day b'pk	O&B	Moderate	8
H5. Holua-Kapalaoa	Side trip	Semiloop	Strenuous	6
H6. Halemauu-Paliku	3-day b'pk	O&B	Strenuous	20⅔
H7. Paliku-Boundary	Side trip	O&B	Strenuous	8
H8. Leleiwi Overlook	Dayhike	O&B	Very Easy	⅓
H9. Kalahaku Overlook	Dayhike	Loop	Very easy	⅙
H10. White Hill	Dayhike	O&B	Easy	½
H11. Rock Garden	Dayhike	O&B	Moderate	2
H12. Ka Luu o Ka Oo	Dayhike	O&B	Strenuous	4¾
H13. Sliding Sands-Kapalaoa	Dayhike	O&B	Strenuous	12½+
	2-day b'pk	O&B	Moderate	12½+
H14. Kapalaoa-Holua	Side trip	Semiloop	Strenuous	8⅔
H15. Slidling Sands-Paliku	2-day b'pk	O&B	Strenuous	19½
H16. Sliding Sands-Halemauu	Dayhike	Shuttle	Strenuous	13
H17. Grand Crater Tour	3-day b'pk	Shuttle	Strenuous	20
H18. Red Hill	Dayhike	Loop	Very easy	—

Trip W1

Waihee Ridge

Distance	Elevation gain	Hiking time	Topos
4½ miles	1500′	2½ hours	Wailuku 7½′

Difficulty: *Moderate, hiking boots strongly recommended.*

Highlights: *On this route, you ascend from pasturelands to a ridge that reaches into the rainforest of the West Maui Mountains. Native plants abound along the upper part of the trail. Weather permitting, several points offer sweeping views over Waihee Valley and the isthmus, even to the western slopes of Haleakala. An early-morning start may put you at the top here before the clouds roll in.*

Driving instructions: From Wailuku (intersection of High Street (Highway 30) and Main Street (Highway 32) drive 2 short blocks east

on Main Street to Market Street, where you turn left (north). Market Street is a one-way street (for northbound traffic) for the next few blocks. Follow Market Street down through Old Wailuku and uphill as it becomes Highway 330 to a Y-junction with Highway 340. Bear left (northwest) on Highway 340 through Waihee town; look for the school on your left. At 6¾ miles from Wailuku and 2.6 miles beyond the school, where you'll see on the road's seaward side an imposing rock wall with a gate signed Mendes Ranch, you turn inland (left) through a gate (unlocked 8 A.M.-6 P.M.) onto a potholed 1-lane road to Camp Mahulia (a Boy Scout camp). Follow this road as it winds uphill for about ⅘ mile. Where the road bears right to Camp Mahulia, you should bear slightly left, off the road and up a small rise to a fence. Park near the fence, but don't block the gate. The trailhead is a few yards to the right of the gate.

Permit/permission required: None

Description: Squeeze through the hiker's pass-through. Near the fence you may notice some bush-sized plants with globular yellow fruit. This is the deadly poisonous apple of Sodom, not the edible guava! Ahead of you, up the slope and southwest, the trail is first a dirt road and then a steep concrete road; stick to it for the time being. The pasture is private property; the road is a right-of-way through it.

In ⅕ mile, near the top of the climb and opposite a water tank, veer left across the road, as indicated by a small sign, and pick up an obvious, grassy track that continues southwest up the slope toward a small wood of swamp mahogany, while the paved road levels out and curves right. Just as you start uphill again, look to your right (west-northwest) across Christmas berry and *kukui* trees for waterfalls plunging from the next major ridge.

At the ¼-mile marker, you enter a dense forest of guava and *kukui*. Soon you reach a locked gate, which you circumvent by scrambling down some slippery, muddy rocks to another narrow hiker's pass-through. Now you get to scramble back up to the road on some more slippery, muddy rocks on the other side. A few Norfolk pines grace the left side of the road here. Stay on the road and ignore a track that leaves the road going uphill on your left.

At a saddle the trail bears right (north-northwest) through guava and strawberry guava, emerging amid eucalyptuses just before the ½ mile marker. It's a single-track trail now, and you soon make a long

View from Waihee Ridge

switchback leg as you climb a hill. At the switchback turn, the water-falls you saw earlier are even more visible. Ahead, there's a wonderful viewpoint—and maybe even a bench—overlooking the isthmus. Just past ¾ mile, you have your first good view into the deep slash of Waihee Valley and into the steep gullies in its southern rim, their dark-green forest canopies slashed by the brash light green of *kukui*. (To hike in the Waihee Valley, see Trip W2.)

Now you dip across a long saddle to another hiker's pass-through—the last one, thank goodness. Beyond here a pattern emerges: you make a few switchbacks, contour across a slope for a while, then switchback again.

You're soon climbing, and you may need a spider stick here. Stair-steps help you up some of the steeper, potentially muddy slopes. In wet weather, huge land snails swim slowly across the damp trail, which is framed by ferns and by the handsome, native *ohia* tree. Look for the red *apapane* bird in this shrubbery. The trail becomes narrow, steep, and slippery here, but there's a fine panorama over West Maui's northwest coast and isthmus.

You cross a narrow saddle around 1½ mile, climb a razorback ridge on "stairs," switchback up a knob, and then traverse the knob's west side through some paperbark eucalyptuses and Norfolk pines. Soon you descend slightly through tall, purple-flowered weeds and squish across a muddy track through a meadow to the next hill west. Here, you contour, climb, and switchback again, passing some mountain *naupaka* shrubs and *kanawao* plants (the native hydrangea) as you go. Tall sedges and branched ferns appear. *Ieie*, a vine whose leaf clusters make it look like a series of miniature palm trees, twines up dwarfed *ohia* trees, and the going can be very muddy.

At the top of the hill, "Lanilili 2563" on the topo, you reach a small, grassy area with a picnic table and an END OF TRAIL sign. Weather permitting, there are far-ranging views from this little summit; look for high waterfalls deep in the misty canyons of West Maui's mountains—maybe even for a view of Molokai, according to a reader. But it's more likely that the clouds will have closed in around you, leaving you alone in this silent, rain forest world. Wait a few minutes; maybe the clouds will part. In either case, you'll enjoy taking a rest and having a snack here.

When you're ready, return the way you came.

Bad guys in the brush

Non-native, invading plants you'll pass as you cross the pasture include the little "bashful plant" with its small, pink powderpuff blossoms and tiny, ferny leaves that fold shut when you stroke them. A real hiker's pest is a clover with tiny, innocent, cherry-pink blossoms and strings of tiny, not-so-innocent, sticky seeds which you will find in abundance on your boots and socks at the end of this trip. Try to pick them all off and leave them here before you drive away. Spikes of blue-flowered cayenne vervain wave amidst the grasses, too. Copses of the Christmas berry tree dot the slopes; look for its seasonal clusters of tiny red, inedible berries. Finally, you can't help but notice clumps of that aggressive invader lantana, with its brilliant pink, orange, and yellow blossoms, rough, dark green leaves, and thorny limbs. Bashing through lantana—not yet necessary on this trip—is a hiker's nightmare. Even if you succeed in making your way through it, lantana will leave bare arms and legs so scratched that they look like street maps and will leave clothing and skin covered with its strong, herbal fragrance.

Trip W2

Waihee Valley

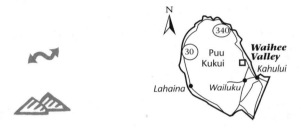

Distance	Elevation gain	Hiking time	Topos
4¼ miles	370′	2+ hours	Wailuku 7½′

Difficulty: *Moderate, hiking boots strongly recommended.*

ALERT: *Vandalizing cars is so rampant here that you may as well resign yourself to it. Leave nothing in the car that you can't afford to lose. Leave the windows cracked and the doors and trunk unlocked in the hope that the thieves will at least not trash the car. Sometimes you will find locals who will let you park in their yards here. If you do, be sure to take them up on it and to offer them a tip for their trouble and your convenience.*

Highlights: *This may be the best of the rainforest stream-valley walks on Maui. The luxuriant, exotic forest and tricky footbridge crossings treat you to a fine combination of beauty, novelty, and excitement. Don't forget your jungle juice and rain gear: Waihee Valley is Mosquito Central and very rainy.*

Driving instructions: Follow the driving instructions of Trip W1 to Waihee town; look for the school on your left as you pass through town. Turn left (inland) onto Waihee Valley Road just over ½ mile past the school. Follow Waihee Valley Road for another ½ mile or less and park in the residential area off the road and *not* blocking anyone's driveway, just over 4½ miles from Wailuku.

Permit/permission required: From Wailuku Agribusiness; see "Getting Permits or Permission" on pages 6–8.

Description: Walk up the road through the residential area to a T-junction with a dirt road, where this trip starts. Turn right (west) to a large gate barring the road. Circumvent the gate via a hiker's pass-through and follow the road past *mao*, reeds, guavas, and Koster's curse. An irrigation ditch, mostly hidden by the shrubbery, bubbles along downhill on your right, bringing water to some taro patches. *Lilikoi* vines festoon some trees, morning-glory vines others. Ignore the side road a little beyond ¹⁄₁₀ mile. Your road soon becomes very rocky and potholed; if it has rained recently, there may be huge puddles to get around. This road continues up the valley, though the topo shows it swinging south.

You cross a dry streambed and bear west-northwest uphill under *kukui* and swamp mahogany trees to a rain gauge. Here the road bears west again, and near ⅓ mile you pass a couple of defunct cable gates. Ferns abound here, sword fern on your left, sweet fern downhill on your right.

Nearing ½ mile, you level out at an open spot; ahead, there's a steep gully—lower Waihee Valley—filled with *kukui* trees, swamp mahogany, yellow strawberry quava, Christmas berry, and huge, spiky sisals. On your left, the irrigation ditch flows through a tunnel under Java plum and Christmas berry trees. Soon the road reaches a locked gate. Hop over the gate or swing around the posts and then follow the road northwest along the ditch. In the next ½ mile, you pass mango trees, ginger plants, and some banyan trees with spectacular roots. The road twists west and northwest, sometimes along the ditch, and always above the river, which is mostly hidden by the rainforest vegetation.

At last, near 1 mile, the rocky riverbed comes into view about 30 feet below. "Cathedral columns" of banyan roots rise on the uphill (left) side of the road. You hop across the ditch where it flows across the road and presently reach the first of Waihee Valley's swinging foot-

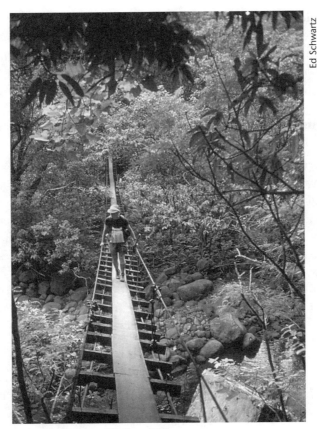

Ed Schwartz

Swinging bridge, Waihee Valley

bridges. Because of the way the irrigation system diverts water, the riverbed may be dry at this point. Still, who can pass up a chance to cross a bridge that's straight out of an Indiana Jones epic? Carefully climb the stairs to gain the wire-cable-and-plank bridge. You'll want to hold on tightly as you cross, because not only does the narrow tread bounce as you go, but it's noticeably tilted to one side. Watch out for frayed wire ends protruding from the cables you hold onto; they can inflict nasty cuts. Descend carefully on the other side, where there are no steps down from the bare bridge support. But there are lots of stones wrapped in leaves—offerings from travelers grateful for a safe crossing.

Bear left (southwest) into the forest on a narrow track that winds along the bank of a tributary. The next swinging bridge is just a few

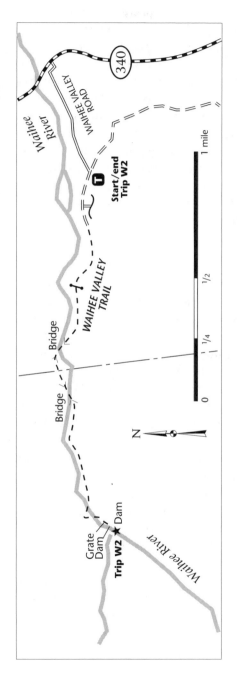

minutes down the trail. Over the bridge and on the other side now, you bear northwest into the forest on the path from the end of the bridge. Bamboo thickets often line one side or the other of the river along this stretch. At a T-junction at 1⅓ miles (not shown on the map), you turn left (west; uphill); the right branch is a spur trail to the river. It's worth your while to pause at open spots to look for cascades high on the lush green walls across the river.

You reach a spot where you have to ford the river—not dry here—on some extremely slippery boulders. Beyond the ford, you bear southwest into the forest under arches of *hau* and past riverbank bamboo thickets. You soon ford the river again near 1¾ miles, where banyans shade pools upstream and downstream. Across the river, you briefly follow a dry, very rocky streambed to a footpath that goes steeply up on your left a short way, past some elaborate tree roots, and levels out as a muddy track. The track soon climbs again to meet the dry channel of an out-of-use ditch. Under a canopy of *kukui*, the track briefly follows the ditch, crosses a streambed, and, almost abreast of a ruined shed, passes some old flow-control machinery for the ditch system. A spur trail leads right to an overlook of a low dam topped by a grate on which fallen guavas may be trapped.

As the vegetation thins, you see the Waihee River foaming along on your right. Just beyond the 2-mile point, one short, steep, downhill pitch and a few level yards bring you to the foot of a dam and to the end of the trail. There are a few spots to plop down for lunch here, and a deep pool below the dam makes a fine swimming hole. The steep concrete wall that descends from the trail to the pool has iron brackets set into it to form a ladder to help you get in and out of the pool.

When you're through with your lunch and swim, return the way you came. Ideally, you'd have views down the valley to the ocean on your way back, but the vegetation is too dense for that.

The Rainy Side

Rainwater coursing down the sides of a volcano has created streams that have cut the many canyons you see as you drive around Maui. Logic tells you that the greater volume of water falling on the rainy side of a volcano ought cut more and bigger canyons than on the dry side. Yet here on the rainy side of West Maui, there are fewer deep stream canyons than there are on the dry, leeward side of West Maui. What could account for the difference?

• According to *Maui: How It Came To Be*, it's the relative hardness or softness of the lavas, not the volume of the streams, that makes the difference on West Maui. The lavas of West Maui's second period of volcanism are harder than those of its initial period of volcanism. The rainy side is covered with a veneer of those harder lavas; the dry side is not. The veneer on the rainy side resists erosion better than the softer material from the initial period, which is exposed on the dry side. That's why the rainy side of West Maui is visibly less eroded than the dry side. On the dry side, the smaller streams have eroded the softer material to create an exotic landscape of deep tropical valleys separated by narrow ridges, of broad alluvial plains, and of one magnificent beach after another—a breathtaking sight!

Trip W3

Halekii-Pihana *Heiau* State Monument

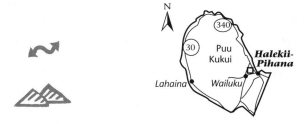

Distance	Elevation gain	Hiking time	Topos
⅖ mile	Negligible	13 minutes	*Wailuku 7½'* (Optional)

Difficulty: *Very easy, tennis shoes recommended.*

Highlights: *Halekii-Pihana Heiau (temple) State Monument has been overlooked by visitors, judging by its state of neglect, but it has features of geological and historical interest, as you'll see. It offers some fine views over the isthmus, too; just ignore the light-industrial areas surrounding the monument. Early in the morning on a clear day, you can see Haleakala from top to bottom from here, backlit against the eastern sky.*

Driving instructions: This one's hard to find, which may be one reason it's so neglected. You can't get there directly from Wailuku, no matter what it looks like on the road map. Instead, you need to take a rather circuitous route. Follow the driving instructions of Trip W1 as far as the junction with Highway 340. Here, turn right onto Highway 340, back toward Wailuku and Kahului. Just as the road begins to climb a little, turn right on Kuhio Place. Go a couple of blocks to Hea Place (there's a very faded Hawaii Visitors Bureau sign on the corner), turn left onto Hea Place, and wind up the short, steep road through the gate to the parking area, 3½ miles from Wailuku. The monument is open from 7 A.M. to 7 P.M., but it's best to come early in the morning. Local people enjoy having lunch up here and socializing here later on. The parking lot can be jam-packed then!

Permit/permission required: None.

Description: An asphalt-paved trail leads south away from the parking lot, but the first feature you'll want to see is at the south end of the lot to the right of the trailhead. Look at the delicate layering pattern exposed in the low, sandy cliff face here. How fragile these thin layers are, almost crumbling into loose sand under the pressure of your gaze. What you're seeing is a cross-section of a lithified sand dune— that's right, a sand dune turned to stone! Much of the isthmus is covered with similar sand dunes, which generally consist of a stony crust and an unconsolidated interior (see below for more on how they formed). Many years ago, your view from here would have swept across sand dunes covered with *kiawe* trees instead of homes and factories. The dunes yield readily to the bulldozer's blade, as you can see in nearby construction sites.

Climb steeply but briefly on the paved path to the top of Halekii *Heiau*, where there's a bare cement circle for a now-missing water tank. Halekii *Heiau* was restored under the direction of anthropologists from the Bishop Museum in 1958. The path becomes a dirt trail now, and a few *milo* and *hala* trees dot the barren plateau. Stray to your left to look down the slope, where elaborate, chambered stone terraces descend to Iao Stream some 160 feet below. According to *Maui: How It Came To Be*, a meander of Iao Stream is gradually undercutting the hill on which these massive structures stand, and eventually they will collapse into its gully. Across an intervening gully to the southeast, you'll see a huge, triangular, stonework wall of Pihana *Heiau* exposed. The great boulders it's made of weigh about 3 times as much as a full-grown adult, yet they are fitted snugly together here without mortar—a work of great skill and dedication.

Follow the path south across a ridge, descending very slightly. The path, as wide as a road here, turns left (east) as you reach a ridge that connects it with the ridge Pihana *Heiau* is on. Look for more evidence of lithified sand dunes along here. *Koa haole* forms thickets from which your approach may flush game birds; *kiawe* trees spread their feathery leaves over the ruins of Pihana and fill the gully below it. In the grass around you, you'll find *mao* (a wild, native relative of cotton), Chinese violets, and a passionflower vine called love-in-a-mist. (Lacy bracts covering buds and fruits distinguish this passionflower from its larger relatives like the edible *lilikoi* and the pesky banana passionflower.)

Now the path bears left (east) and a little uphill to Pihana's simple marker. From here, you can turn left again and walk north a few more steps to the top of the triangular wall you admired from Halekii for a different view of it and for fine views of the landscape.

Return the way you came. Driving back, you'll probably notice other lithified sand dunes exposed by the road cuts. (Also when driving back, you'll need to dodge left or right to avoid the one-way segment of Market Street.)

Lithified *Whats?*

Of all the things that might turn to stone, a sand dune seems one of the least likely. What are sand dunes of this size and extent doing here between two volcanoes, anyway? The dunes rest on lava flows from Haleakala which have piled up against West Maui. And, according to *Maui: How It Came To Be*, the dunes are in a way the work of the great, far-away glaciers of the Ice Ages. Each Ice Age lowered the level of the oceans by locking water up in glaciers. The lower ocean level exposed wide, sandy beaches at the isthmus. Trade winds piled the sand over the isthmus "into long ridges, sorting it into coarse and fine layers." Plants took root on the dunes, anchoring them. Carbonic acid from the roots dissolved a constituent of the sand, calcium carbonate, which is insoluble in water. The dissolved calcium percolated through the layers, changing as it went back to calcium carbonate, which is a natural cement and which bound the sand grains together. It was this cementing process that produced the stony layers. Beneath them, as you can see, less-cemented sand now exposed to weathering has fallen away from the stony part to form pockets where new plants can grow.

The shield volcanoes of Maui, Molokai, Lanai, and Kahoolawe meet at relatively shallow depths in the sea now. It's believed that when the ocean level was lower during the Ice Ages, the four islands were joined above sea level to form an island, called Maui-nui, which would have been about half the size of the present Big Island of Hawaii. On all the islands, erosional features attributed to wave action now lie below as well as above present sea level. They're interpreted as testifying to higher as well as lower sea levels than at present—and to the power of glaciers far to the north to reshape these tropical islands.

Trip W4

Kanaha Pond

Distance	Elevation gain	Hiking time	Topos
Negligible	Negligible	Less than 5 minutes	*Wailuku 7½', Paia 7½' (Optional)*

Difficulty: Very easy, tennis shoes recommended.

Highlights: Waterfowl, especially in the winter, when Kanaha Pond is home for many migratory birds. Birders will want to bring their binoculars and guides along.

Driving instructions: From Wailuku, drive east on Highway 32 past Maui Community College to the point where the main highway bears southeast (right) to become Highway 36 (the Hana Highway).

Stay in the left lane here, because in a few blocks you'll bear left (east) onto Haleakala Road where a sign says this is the way to Kahului Airport. You'll be on Haleakala Road for barely a block. As you head toward the airport, you'll notice a large, fenced, undeveloped area on your left. Look for a barely visible turnoff to the left into the undeveloped area. It's hard to spot in time; if you reach the junction with Highway 380, you've gone too far, so turn around as best you can—and go back. There's a small parking lot here for Kanaha Pond's observation shelter, 3⅓ miles from Wailuku.

Permit/permission required: None.

Description: Walk through the gate (be sure to close it) and out to the observation shelter, about 100 yards. The concrete benches here are not particularly comfortable, but the shelter does help conceal your presence. Ignore the occasional roar of airplane engines and the smell of jet fuel as you concentrate on watching the birds.

Retrace your steps to your car.

Of Stilts and Coots and Such

Year-round residents include noisy, black-necked stilts (aeo) with red legs and in black and white plumage so formal-looking as to rival that of the "tuxedo-clad" penguin; plump, white-beaked coots (*alae ke okeo*, close relatives of the "mudhens" from whom, according to Hawaiian legend, the demigod Maui stole the secret of fire); and black-crowned night-herons (*aukuu*), the juveniles of which are brown with white streaks.

Birds are more numerous in the winter, when many migratory species winter over here. Still, a visit at any time is rewarding and educational. I watched a young night-heron stand so still for so long, not even blinking, that I decided it was a decoy stuck into the mud to attract other birds. A black-necked stilt came poke-poke-poking along through the mud almost to the motionless heron's feet—yes, that heron was a decoy—and *fwoom!* the heron snapped back to life and flapped away.

On my latest visit, I enjoyed watching a handsome stilt moving gracefully from hummock to hummock as it hunted, and I chuckled at the antics of a couple of crabby, squabbling mudhens—the phrase "mad as a wet hen" came irresistibly to mind.

Trip W5

Kepaniwai County Park

Distance	Elevation gain	Hiking time	Topos
⅔ mile	Negligible	20 minutes	*Wailuku 7½'* (Optional)

Trail map: No particular route shown, so many are possible.

Difficulty: Very easy, tennis shoes recommended.

Highlights: Kepaniwai County Park, in beautiful Iao Valley, offers a unique opportunity to remember the people who immigrated to Hawaii long ago. The park also offers plenty of pavilions where you can picnic.
   Don't miss the Hawaii Nature Center in Iao Valley near Kepaniwai County Park. This teaching center includes an interactive nature-arcade tour (fee) especially designed for instructing children about Hawaii's environment and delightful for adults, too. Hawaii Nature Center personnel lead daily hikes (fee) in Iao Valley. Write or call in advance for more

information; include a SASE. They're at 875 Iao Valley Road, Wailuku, Maui, HI 96793, (808) 244-6500.

Driving instructions: From the intersection of Main Street (Highway 32) and High Street (Highway 30) in downtown Wailuku, drive west (toward the mountains) on Main Street, past the Maui Historical Society Museum ("Bailey House"). At a fork in the road, take the right fork slightly downhill to the turn-in (on your left) for Kepaniwai Park, just over 2 miles from downtown Wailuku.

Permit/permission required: None.

Description: The principal feature of Kepaniwai County Park is a series of "pavilions"—gardens, paths, streams, miniature homes, and

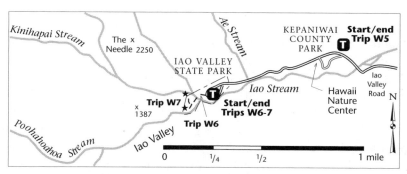

Overview: Kepani County Park and Iao Valley State Park

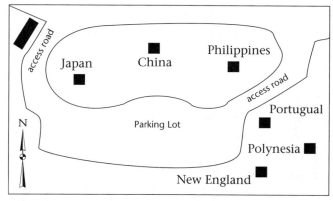

Close-up: Kepani County Park (not to scale)

Garden path, Kepaniwai Park

monuments—in honor of the major ethnic groups that settled in Hawaii over the past 1700 years: Polynesians, people of Northern European descent (New England missionaries), Chinese, Japanese, Portuguese, and Filipinos. You can wander along the pleasant maze of walkways and waterways, across miniature bridges, and past simple replicas of typical houses as long as you wish. If you belong to a group represented here, you may wish to go to that "pavilion" first in honor of your ethnic kin; see the map following this trip. Or you may prefer simply to stroll along, appreciating this pretty little park and its monuments. You'll certainly want to spend more time here than the distance given above would suggest. When you're ready to leave, you'll probably just make a beeline for your car, as the parking lot is more or less central to the park.

Step Back in History

You may want to try this exercise in historical imagination. Walk to each "pavilion" in turn and imagine yourself in the place of someone emigrating from that land to distant Hawaii over a hundred or more years ago. Stand near the door of the

Kaahumanu Church

miniature house. Imagine that it's your home, which you are leaving forever, as far as you know. At least 2000 miles of open, wild ocean lie between you and a strange land called Hawaii. What draws you to Hawaii? Are you pulled toward Hawaii by hope for a better life, by a love of adventure, or by a commitment to saving souls? Or are you pushed toward Hawaii by hopeless conditions at home, by banishment, or by a vow to follow someone else? Friends and relatives whom you will never see or hear again call farewell to you; you try in these last few minutes to fix their faces in your memory. But the ship is ready to sail; you can wait no longer. You pick up your few belongings, take a deep breath, and walk away toward your new life.

Battle of Kepaniwai

Life in old Hawaii was far from peaceful. In 1790, Kahekili, king of Maui, was trying to conquer Oahu as part of his plan to conquer all the islands. He had left his son Kalanikupule to rule Maui in his absence. Kahekili was well on his way to achieving his objective, but he wasn't the only ambitious chief. The chief who would ultimately succeed in ruling all the islands, Kamehameha, attacked Maui in Kahekili's absence. With the help of European guns, Kamehameha defeated Kalanikupule here at Kepaniwai. So fierce and bloody was the battle of Kepaniwai that the corpses dammed Iao Stream. Kalanikupule escaped from Kamehameha this time, fleeing up Iao Valley, over the ridge, and down to Olowalu. They would meet again.

Kahekili wrested Maui away from Kamehameha and was king of all the islands but Hawaii—for a while. He soon lost control of Kauai and Niihau. After old Kahekili died, the islands were divided between Kalanikupule and Kahekili's younger brother, Kaeo. Kalanikupule and Kaeo coveted each other's share of Kahekili's islands, and soon they were at war. Needing modern weapons, Kalanikupule enlisted the help of Americans and Europeans, including the services of two British ships. With their aid, he defeated Kaeo's forces on Oahu, killing Kaeo in the battle. Now Kalanikupule became ambitious to oust Kamehameha from the Big Island and to rule all the islands. He thought he could do so if he controlled those fine British ships and their weapons, so he murdered the ships' captains and took the crews as prisoners. Kamehameha learned of Kalanikupule's plans when the ships' crews rebelled and fled to the Big Island, and, before sailing for China, presented Kamehameha with the ships' armaments and apprised him of Kalanikupule's plots. Kamehameha pursued his rival, conquering first Maui and then Molokai. He caught up with Kalanikupule on Oahu and defeated him at the terrible battle of Nuuanu Pali in 1795. Kalanikupule escaped once more and wandered in the mountains of Oahu for some months before he was captured and sacrificed to Kamehameha's war god.

Iao Valley State Park: Nature Trail

Distance	Elevation gain	Hiking time	Topos
¼ mile	60' (Loss/gain)	Less than 10 minutes	*Wailuku 7½'* (Optional)

Difficulty: *Very easy, tennis shoes recommended.*

Highlights: *This pleasant trail takes you down through handsome tropical plants to Iao Stream. As of this writing, many of the plants are identified by signs at their bases, giving you a chance to learn the names of some of the non-native landscaping plants and a few of the native plants you'll see around Maui.*

71

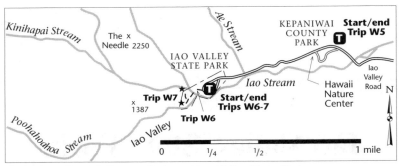

Overview: Kepani County Park and Iao Valley State Park

Close-up: Iao Valley State Park (not to scale)

Iao Valley State Park is justly famous for its great beauty and draws many visitors. Often, its parking lot overflows by midday. The park's gates are open from 7 A.M. to 7 P.M. Be there around 7 A.M. to avoid the crowds (trust me: it's worth the trouble). Whatever else you do on Maui, I hope you'll make time for Iao Valley State Park!

Driving instructions: Follow the driving instructions of Trip W5 past Kepaniwai Park (on your left) to Iao Valley State Park, 2⅕ miles, at the end of the road.

Permit/permission required: None.

Description: From the end of the parking lot, walk west on the asphalt trail past the restrooms and drinking fountain. Trees and

Clockwise from above: torch ginger, *kukui*, octopus tree

shrubs bordering the path include *kukui*, octopus tree, strawberry guava, and yellow ginger. Look for red and orange heliconia "blossoms" downslope on your left; the "blossoms" are actually the colorful bracts of the inconspicuous flowers. Just before you'd cross a footbridge, an asphalt path branches left (southwest), descending. Follow that path downhill past royal poinciana trees, angel's-trumpet trees, torch ginger, yellow heliconia, and many more splendid tropical plants. Some of them are sure to be in bloom while you're there, no matter when you visit! Soon you're at the loop portion of the trail (see the map close-up), where you wander around and through the loop as you wish. Where the loop touches the streambank, there are wonderful views along Iao Stream, especially upstream to some cascasdes.

Close the loop when you've seen enough, and retrace your steps to your car if you're "hiked out." It's certainly feasible for most people to continue to the Needle Overlook (Trip W7). Sturdy, experienced, properly equipped hikers will have no trouble taking all the Iao Valley State Park hikes in this book (Trips W6 and W7) in one day or less.

Trip W7

Iao Valley State Park: Needle Overlook and Streamside Loop

Distance	Elevation gain	Hiking time	Topos
1½ miles	200'	½+ hour	*Wailuku 7½'* (Optional)

Difficulty: *Easy, tennis shoes recommended.*

Highlights: *A close-up view of West Maui's most famous scenic attraction, Iao Needle. Afterwhich, you descend to one of the park's streams and enjoy a pretty streamside walk through a lush tropical landscape.*

Iao Needle

Driving instructions: Follow the driving instructions of Trip W6.

Permit/permission required: None.

Description: If you're a card-carrying couch potato, you can get a pretty decent view of Iao Needle from the end of the parking lot and let it go at that. But you'll probably want to see more of it, so follow Trip W6 to the trail junction just before the footbridge. The footbridge takes you safely across a tributary of Iao Stream. The bridge offers a wonderful view of the Needle. On the other side of the stream, curve left on the paved path. (The sign you may notice pointing to the right here does not point out a trail; it's pointing out the Needle to you, as if you hadn't already figured out that that big green thing *is* Iao Needle.)

Iao Stream

The path climbs slightly past *ti*, giant philodendron, guava, and plumeria, quickly reaching a junction where a narrow side trail branches left (down). You bear right at this fork, a pleasant turn-out on the left where you'll find benches and an interpretive sign about the Battle of Kepaniwai. Continue climbing, now on stairs, toward the overlook. The going gets steeper, and there's an opportunity partway up the stairs to stop, rest, and enjoy the view. Climbing again, you soon reach the overlook with its shelter, benches, and pavilion. What wonderful views

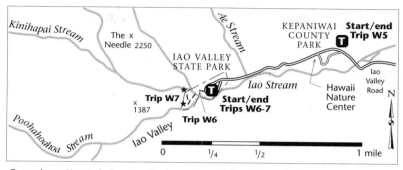

Overview: Kepani County Park and Iao Valley State Park

Close-up: Iao Valley State Park (not to scale)

you have from here, just over ¹/₁₀ mile from the parking lot! You can see northwest toward Iao Needle, east down Iao Valley, and south toward the steep valley walls.

From the Needle Overlook retrace your steps to the last junction you passed as you came up. Turn right at this fork and almost immediately turn right again onto a trail that leads down to the stream. Descend on this trail under Christmas berry and guava, past fragrant yellow ginger, to a lovely overlook of the stream. An unpaved path signed NO TRESPASSING branches west (right) away from this point. Curve left here, toward the stream.

Continue ahead (right), descending, on the paved trail past mango and *kukui* to the confluence of two of the Park's streams. Curve around to the left on the paved trail, pausing to enjoy the scenery. There are some especially photo-worthy views upstream to Iao Needle and the footbridge. However, if you are tempted to scramble out onto one of the midstream boulders for a photo of the Needle, be aware that getting out there and back can be difficult, especially if your shoes don't have soles that grip when wet. You, your camera, and that great shot may go for an unscheduled swim.

Now the trail climbs steadily up toward the footbridge and the junction with the main trail. At that junction, turn right and retrace your steps to the parking lot.

What is Iao Needle?

The rocky material a volcano produces isn't uniform. Its mineral composition varies from one eruption to the next, so that cooled lava from one eruption may be harder than that from another eruption of the same volcano. Sometimes the lava is deposited as a flow, becoming dense and hard when it cools. Other times, it's spewed out as ash or clinker, small particles which may consolidate with time and with pressure from overlying material into a layer that is relatively soft and easily eroded. Older volcanic material cracks as it's stressed by later geological events. Newer, fluid lavas can invade these cracks, forming "dikes" of tough rock that can actually strengthen the older material.

Iao Needle is a lump of older material from the first phase of volcanic activity of West Maui. Later eruptions strengthened what would become Iao Needle by filling its cracks with numerous, newer dikes. When streams flowing down Puu Kukui's slopes scoured out Iao Valley from the old volcano's softer material, Iao Needle and its ridge withstood the streams' cutting forces. At 2250 feet high, Iao Needle now stands over 1200 feet above the valley floor. The streams long ago deposited the softer material as alluvium at the mouth of Iao Valley or carried it out to sea. Iao Needle appears to be a spire because from the park, you see its narrow southeast edge. From most other directions, it's the last big hump on a small, steep ridge which has several other humps.

Who's (or what's) that on the trail?

Besides the true wildlife, company you may have on most trails can include other hikers, hunters and their dogs, feral animals (goats and pigs), and lost hunting dogs. Be alert for vehicles when your trail is actually a road. Many trails on Maui pass through areas where hunting is legal. (The occasional terrible stench from some unidentifiable source may be a carcass rotting in the forest.)

You'll have to use your own judgment about how to handle what you meet. Here are some things that worked for me: You should *always* stay on established routes, trails, or roads in order to avoid being mistaken for a game animal. If you meet lost hunting dogs, try what one hunter advised me: tell them firmly, "Go home." Wild goats are very alert and shy; you can't get close to them. It's possible you'll surprise wild pigs rooting along the trail. Slow your pace to give them time to get away. Give vehicles the right-of-way.

Walking Upstream

It's tempting to walk in the streambed when the trail is blocked, but that's not a good idea. Streambeds and their boulders are often very slippery, so you're risking injury if you try to hike up them. You may also find the water surprisingly deep and swift. Rain can quickly swell these streams (and all Hawaiian streams) to flood proportions. If the stream begins to rise, get away from it before you're caught in a flash flood! Finally, Iao Valley State Park is quite small. You are trespassing if you continue upstream beyond the end of a trail in Iao Valley State Park.

Trip W8

Maalaea Beach

Distance	Elevation gain	Hiking time	Topos
4 miles	Negligible	2 hours	Maalaea 7½' (Optional)

Trail map: There's no trail as such; you just follow the shoreline.

Difficulty: Moderate, tennis shoes recommended.

Highlights: Maalaea (locally pronounced "mah-LY-ah") Bay, sometimes called "the nursery of the humpback whales," is a prime whale-watching spot during the winter months. Its long, narrow beach is presently unbroken by buildings for 2 miles and offers great views of Kahoolawe and of West or East Maui (Haleakala), depending on the direction you're walking. Wear tennis shoes or sandals you don't mind getting wet, so you can splash in the water if the surf's calm. This is best as a morning walk. By midday, the normal strong breezes will drive sand against you *with stinging force, which is why you rarely see sunbathers on Maalaea Beach. (If it's not as windy as usual, consider making this a sunset hike. Sunset over West Maui from here can be a glorious spectacle!)*

Driving instructions: From Wailuku, drive south on Highway 30 for 5 miles to the junction with Highway 31, which goes southeast to Kihei. Turn left onto Highway 31 and drive about 3⅓ miles. On the left, you pass a power plant and Kealia Pond; on the right, you pass mud flats and then a narrow beach backed by *kiawe* trees. This hike starts at the southeast end of that beach, near the northernmost condominium building in Kihei. As you near that building, look on the beach side of the road for a spot where you can safely park. A sailing club uses the very last spot, right next to the condo building, so pick one a little earlier.

Permit/permission required: None.

Description: You're probably parked just a few steps from the beach. Thread your way along any of the many paths worn through the dunes and *kiawe* trees to the beach. Once you're at the water's edge,

Maalaea Bay

Maui Trails

Maalaea Bay

pause to enjoy the magnificent views and to snap a few photos. East and West Maui are so huge as seen from here, and the isthmus so low and inconspicuous, that it's easy to imagine for a moment that East and West Maui are separate islands.

Now turn right toward West Maui (northwest) and begin your walk along this strand. There may be some abandoned junk back in the dunes, perhaps even some illegal campsites, but you can ignore them and concentrate on the beauty of this bay. Depending on the tide conditions, the beach may become so narrow at places that you'll need to walk on the stony shelves of beach rock or in the water. (If the surf is rough, stay out of the water!) The beach rock forms some lovely, clear, pale-blue tide pools, and you'll probably see people fishing here. However, the beach rock can be slippery and sharp, so keep your shoes on and watch your step.

Just beyond the 1-mile point, two parallel lines of black boulders and some old remnants of a wharf extend toward the sea from an arm of Kealia Pond. Birders may want to detour inland here, especially in winter, when many migratory birds stop at Kealia Pond. The main body of the pond lies across the highway, but you may be able to spot some feathered visitors along this small arm. The mud flats on this side of the highway may have some birds, too, if they are flooded. But people use the flats as a motocross course on the weekends, so they're more likely to be uninteresting, possibly even hazardous. Back on the beach, you get over the boulders and continue your stroll until, at 2 miles, a spit of black boulders and more rusty equipment block your way. The buildings of Maalaea village rise a little beyond these boulders, so it's time to retrace your steps to your car.

Birding at the Ponds

Two large ponds on the isthmus provide places for migratory waterfowl to winter over and for non-migratory waterfowl to live: larger Kealia Pond here on the south side of the isthmus and smaller Kanaha Pond on the north side. Kanaha Pond (Trip W4) is open to the public and developed for birding. Kealia Pond has now been purchased and become a sanctuary open to the public, too, but remains undeveloped. There are plans to construct parking areas, boardwalks, and interpretive aids at Kealia Pond. But for now you must park on the highway's shoulder and follow any of the many use trails that bash their way through the dense weeds surrounding the pond in order to view the birds. Depending on the bird activity at Kealia Pond, a visit can be well worth your trouble.

Trip W9

Lahaina Pali Trail

Distance	Elevation gain	Hiking time	Topos
5 miles	1500'	2½ hours	Maalaea 7½'

Difficulty: *Strenuous, hiking boots strongly recommended.*

Highlights: *An historic carriage road over Kealaloloa Ridge, resurrected as a very rugged hiking trail with love and hard work by a consortium of hiking and outdoor groups, offers you splendid views and a slice of history. Be sure to pick up from the Department of Land and Natural Resources the pamphlet "Tales From the Trail: Maui History and Lore from the Lahaina Pali Trail: A Trail Guide," by Na Ala Hele. It details the road's natural and human history through 16 described points along the route. Take plenty of water: the trail is rocky, exposed, steep in places, and may be hot, and all those gulches are normally dry.*

Driving instructions:

West (Ukumehame) end: From Wailuku, take Highway 30 south and then west through the Lahaina Tunnel, which pierces massive, south-trending Kealaloloa Ridge. Four-tenths of a mile west of the west end of the tunnel, turn right on an obscure dirt road leading into a dirt parking lot under *kiawe* trees. The west end of the Lahaina Pali Trail is at the upper end of this lot, 10.7 miles from Wailuku.

East (Maalaea) end: The eastern (Maalaea) trailhead has been destroyed by what look like flash floods, heavy over-growth, and neglect. For now, there is no Maalaea-side trailhead.

Permit/permission required: None.

Description: Two plaques set in stonework at the back of the Ukumehame-end parking lot provide some background information and show where the trail starts on the edge of Manawaipueo Gulch. Head northwest into the *kiawe* and then veer right (east-southeast) on an old section of pavement. Ascend to fine views of the ocean, the isthmus, Haleakala, Kahoolawe, and Lanai; these views are only going to get better as you climb over Kealaloloa Ridge.

The booklet notes that while the historic road you're following was built almost 200 years ago, it is almost certainly part of an pre-European route that encircled Maui: the *alaloa*, or "long road," much of which tradition says was built by Kiha-a-Piilani, who ruled Maui about 400 years ago. Imagine you're walking this trail in *ti*-leaf sandals, as the ancient Hawaiians did, or rattling over it in a nineteenth-century carriage, feeling as if your bones will be shaken apart at every joint, or, worst of all, being the draft animal that hauls the carriage and its occupants over this road! Looking down at the present road, you can see rockslides over remnants of an older near-sea-level road. It's quite a job to maintain today's road around McGregor and Papawai points!

The trail hooks left (north) off the road abruptly to begin a steep ascent on the signed LAHAINA PALI TRAIL, soon meeting the first numbered marker corresponding to the booklet's notes. This part of the trail roughly parallels the paved road below as it climbs. After a cobblestoned section, the grade eases and views continue to open up.

At ¾ mile, a lone *kiawe* tree shades some welcome, "sittable" boulders far above the tunnel and Kamaohi Gulch. You then dip a bit before climbing around the head of the gulch, which frames a good view of Kahoolawe. The trail is now steep, now gradual, now dirt, now rocks or cobbles—and always with knockout views.

The trail is broad and gradual as it approaches Manawainui Gulch. Colorful plants you may notice here include a yellow aster, the golden *ilima*, blue cayenne vervain, white powderpuffs of *koa haole*, and the *aalii* with its shiny red pods. The soil colors are especially vivid in the sides of deep Manawainui Gulch, the largest of the gulches you'll traverse on this trail.

Climb out of the gulch on a couple of long switchback legs, angling up the ridge on a stony track that becomes an old road. It's not long before you reach the trail's high point at a little over 2½ miles and 1600 feet, where the sweeping panorama embraces Maalaea Bay, Kealia Pond, often-cloud-shrouded Haleakala, Molokini, and Kahoolawe. This is a good place to turn around if you don't plan to go all the way to the Maalaea side.

The descent on the Maalaea side begins gradually, briefly joining a jeep road. As you round the ridge leaving Malalowaiaole Gulch, the trail leaves the jeep road on the right at the ridge nose. A large *kiawe* tree near the Mile-3 marker provides a bit of shade. The trail may be overgrown in places.

Now you zigzag steeply down on loose, rocky footing. At little past the Mile-4 marker, at about 500 feet, at the bottom of a nameless gulch, you enter an area of *kiawe* trees, and their scant shade is welcome, although you lose your views. As you curve away from the gulch, the grade eases, and you presently pass the Mile-4.5 marker before reaching twin plaques mounted in stonework at the Maalaea-side trailhead and parking lot. Retrace your steps to the Ukumehame-side trailhead.

Kahoolawe

Trip W10

Olowalu:
Kilea Cone Petroglyphs

Distance	Elevation gain	Hiking time	Topos
1 mile	80'	½ hour	*Olowalu 7½'* (Optional)

Difficulty: *Easy, tennis shoes recommended.*

Highlights: *Centuries ago, Hawaiians carved drawings of people, animals, and everyday objects into exposed stone faces. Drawings in stone such as these, called petroglyphs, are typical of stone-age societies. Many petroglyph sites exist on Maui, but often they're hard to find or hard to get to. The petroglyphs on an exposed rock face of Kilea cone near Olowalu are in good condition, and you can easily see them on this little hike.*

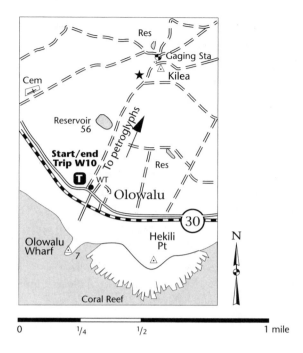

Driving instructions: From Wailuku, drive south on Highway 30. Follow it around McGregor Point to Olowalu village, 15 miles. Olowalu Store is on the inland side of the highway. Turn in here; find a place to park where you won't block any of the dirt roads and aren't taking up room in the store's and restaurant's parking lot. A reader suggests driving just past the "good dirt road" of the description below, then turning left on the road that runs behind the house, store and restaurant. You go through a gate, turn right, and park just outside a gate signed OLOWALU ELUA ASSOCIATES, under trees.

Allow plenty of time for this drive—and for any other drive around to the west side of West Maui. The scenery is spectacular, and you'll want to stop often to enjoy it safely. There are also a number of beautiful public beaches where you'll find it hard to resist the temptation to picnic and swim.

Permit/permission required: None. The new owners, Olowalu Elua Associates, LLC, (808) 877-4204, have posted signs to help you hike.

Description: A good dirt road leads inland (north-northeast) away from the highway and past a house. Follow that road as it rises almost imperceptibly past an old water tower and through canefields. The reservoir you see on the topo is invisible from the road. The irrigation ditch is usually out of sight, too, though you may hear it. The walk can be very hot on a still afternoon, so it would be better to visit the petroglyphs in the morning.

Soon you approach the west face of an old volcanic cone called Kilea 264 on the topo. Smooth, reddish rock is exposed on this face, and here the Hawaiians of long ago have chiseled drawings. Drawings of stylized human figures are particularly prominent. Unfortunately, some of the petroglyphs have been vandalized with spray paint. Shaky stairways can help you get a closer look.

When you've had a good look at the petroglyphs and a chance to photograph them, return the way you came. (Please remember not to go any farther than the petroglyphs.)

A petroglyph of a human figure

The Olowalu Massacre

One of the many tragic episodes of late-eighteenth-century Hawaii took place here at quiet Olowalu village. Coincidentally, that tragedy gave Kamehameha his two most trusted European advisors, the Englishmen Isaac Davis and John Young. An American, Captain Simon Metcalfe of Boston, was the villain.

In his ship the *Eleanora*, Metcalfe sailed first to the Big Island of Hawaii. His son Thomas followed him in a smaller ship, the *Fair American*, and did not reach Hawaii until some weeks after his father. While trading on the Big Island, Simon Metcalfe caught a high chief stealing and, never one for diplomacy, struck the chief with the end of a rope. The chief vowed revenge for the insult, but Simon Metcalfe sailed off to Maui. Someone else would have to suffer the chief's vengeance.

Simon Metcalfe was trading off the coast of Maui at Honuaula in 1790 when some natives stole one of the *Eleanora's* auxiliary boats, killing the crewman in it. Another native tried to pry the copper plating off the bottom of the ship. Metcalfe refused to trade any more. The next day, he fired on Honuaula to drive the natives away and then sent a party ashore to burn the village.

Metcalfe then heard that the boat thieves had come from Olowalu, so he sailed to Olowalu for revenge. He invited the natives there to come out to trade, and scores of natives flocked to the *Eleanora*. The treacherous Metcalfe told the natives that one side of the *Eleanora* was *kapu*. That meant the natives would have to bring all their canoes up to the other side of the ship. And on that side, Metcalfe had placed all his cannons and guns, loaded not with their usual ammunition but with musket balls, nails, and scraps of metal. He waited until the canoes were within range and then fired a broadside that killed at least a hundred natives outright and wounded an estimated two hundred more—the Olowalu massacre.

In the meantime, his son Thomas had reached the Big Island in the *Fair American*. The high chief whom Simon Metcalfe had struck now took his revenge, not knowing that one of his victims was the son of the man who had insulted him. The chief and his men boarded the *Fair American*, seized its crew, and threw them overboard to drown. Only the mate, Isaac Davis, survived after having struggled for so long that the chief finally took pity on him. Kamehameha heard of the attack, chastised the chief, appropriated the *Fair American*, and put Davis under his protection.

Simon Metcalfe sailed back to the Big Island, leaving Olowalu to mourn its dead and heal its wounded. He sent the *Eleanora's* boatswain, John Young, ashore to inquire after the *Fair American* and her crew. Kamehameha, fearing an ugly confrontation, took Young prisoner so he could not report back and put a *kapu* on the *Eleanora* so that Hawaiians could not go out to it and tell Simon Metcalfe what had happened. After days of fruitless waiting, Simon Metcalfe sailed away from Hawaii, still ignorant of his son's fate.

Kamehameha needed Europeans to help him deal with other Europeans and manage the modern weapons he'd acquired. Isaac Davis and John Young had little formal education, but each possessed a great deal of common sense and integrity. They tried to escape Kamehameha but failed; eventually, they agreed to serve him. They served him loyally and well. Their excellence accounted for much of the Hawaiian mon-archy's preference for Great Britain over the United States. Both married Hawaiian women, raised families, and never returned to England. Isaac Davis died of poisoning in 1810; he had helped to foil a plot, and his death was the plotters' revenge. "Old John Young" outlived Kamehameha I by many years; his granddaughter Emma became Kamehameha IV's queen.

D.T. Fleming Beach Park to "Dragon's Teeth"

Distance	Elevation gain	Hiking time	Topos
1¾ miles	Negligible	1 hour	*Napili 7½'*

Difficulty: *Easy, tennis shoes recommended.*

Highlights: *D.T. Fleming Beach Park is a beautiful tropical beach where you're sure to enjoy sunning and picnicking (the surf's a bit rough for swimming, and it's day use only). But the real highlight here is your walk out onto Makaluapuna Point through its unusual trachyte formations that* Maui: How It Came To Be *calls "dragon's teeth."*

Driving instructions: From Wailuku, follow Highway 30 through Lahaina, Kaanapali, and Kapalua. D.T. Fleming Beach Park is adjacent to the huge Kapalua resort development. At the north end of Kapalua, an old coast road joins Highway 30 from the southwest, coming in from the left side (as you're driving north on Highway 30); that's the road you turn onto to get to D.T. Fleming. However, the turnoff to D.T. Fleming is not marked on the highway as of this writing and can be hard to spot. Kapalua has several golf courses; one set brackets the highway south of D.T. Fleming Beach Park; another, north of D.T. Fleming, is on the inland side of the highway. If you are driving north and have passed one set of Kapalua golf courses bracketing the highway; and then, get to a right turn inland into another golf course—and residential development—on the inland side of the highway, you have overshot the old coast road that leads to D.T. Fleming. Turn around and then, as you head back (south), take the next right (seaward) turnoff. Or, if you're northbound and haven't overshot the turnoff, turn left onto the old coast road and go southwest a very short distance to the park entrance. D.T. Fleming Beach Park is on your right (seaward) as you pass a lovely old building on your left that looks like a church but is currently serving as a preschool. The park entrance isn't well-marked either, as of this writing, so don't be surprised if you pass

"Dragon's teeth"

it and have to backtrack. There's a parking lot here with restrooms at its north end, 9 miles past Lahaina and 31 miles from Wailuku.

Permit/permission required: None.

Description: From the parking lot, walk past the restrooms toward the northeast end of the beach, where pretty Honokahua Stream empties into Honokahua Bay under ironwood, *kiawe,* and sisal. Now turn around to enjoy the sweeping view of Honokahua Bay and Makaluapuna Point, which is your destination. Drift back southwest along the shoreline toward the point, dabbling your feet in the water if the surf is calm. In ⅓ mile, the beach ends at the lava rocks of the point.

Carefully pick your way up onto the point, keeping outside the fence of a golf course (not shown on the map). If the tide is high, crashing surf may make this unsafe. Atop the point, you'll find a use trail that leads through a wall of black boulders and through beach *naupaka.* The use trail soon peters out, leaving you to pick your way across the mostly gray-white lavas of Makaluapuna Point. These light-colored lavas are characteristic of the second period of volcanism on West Maui and are poorer in iron than the basalts that originally formed West Maui's shield volcano. They're also sharp; this is no place for bare feet or sandals. Look for a low, white-flowered variety of the succulent plant *akulikuli* trailing across the rocks here.

As you continue out on the east side of the point, you'll notice that salt spray has eroded these rocks into sweeping, sharp "dragon's tooth" shapes—or are they the dragon's backbone? They're almost as tall as a person! Take some time to explore this world of gray, black, and reddish lavas, unexpected grassy flats, and small tide pools. There's a miniature natural arch, far too fragile to step on, over a tiny, deep cove whose wave-battered black lava rocks are stained pink by algae. Near the very end of the point, you'll find rusty pipes set in concrete bases. Pause to look inland. Somewhere up on that slope above Kapalua lies the vent from which these lavas poured, dividing what was once a single long bay into the two bays you see now, Honokahua (from which you just came) on the east and Oneloa on the west.

You can trace your way back on the west side of the point as far as the golf course. The sands of Oneloa Bay are inviting, but you'd have to trespass on the golf course to get there from here. So, when you're through exploring Makaluapuna Point, return to D.T. Fleming Beach Park and to your car.

Trip W12

Nakalele Blowhole

Distance	Elevation gain	Hiking time	Topos
Just under 1 mile	150' (Loss/gain)	½ hour	Napili 7½' (Optional)

Difficulty: *Easy, tennis shoes recommended.*

Highlights: *The blowhole is located in a small, extremely rugged cove, surrounded by fantastically sculpted formations. It's far too rough and dangerous for swimming, but it certainly is picturesque.*

Driving instructions: Don't waste your time driving around the north end of West Maui to get to Nakalele Blowhole (see page 26). You'll see better scenery and have an opportunity to visit many more attractions if you take the highway through Lahaina. From Wailuku, follow Highway 30 through Lahaina, Kaanapali, and Kapalua. Beyond Kapalua, the road narrows and becomes more winding. You'll find the trailhead on the seaward side of the highway some 37⅓ miles from Wailuku. Nakelele is currently signed; turn into the big, bare area on the seaward side of the highway, and park here to start your hike.

Permit/permission required: None.

Description: There are two conflicting signs at the parking area, a NO TRESPASSING sign and a Maui County Parks and Recreation sign. Here's the situation: The public access route, to which the Maui County sign refers, is an old road which you may hike on. The land on either side of the road, to which the NO TRESPASSING sign refers, is private property where you may not go. Stick to the old road as described below.

An old jeep road, far too rough for driving but fine for hiking, bears east away from the parking area, descending a little as it goes. It becomes indistinct at a grassy area, but look to your right (east) for a gully with a stand of ironwood trees. Follow the road toward the gully, which has cut its way across the old road, cross the gully—don't hike up or down it—and then bear left toward the old Nakalele beacon ("Light" on the topo), ⅓ mile.

There's no trail beyond the beacon, so you pick your way down and to your right as you face the sea, to the cove below the beacon. Small piles of rocks indicate routes others have taken, but you should use your own judgement. Be careful to avoid cutting yourself on the sharp rocks and when putting your weight on fragile lava formations that could crumble beneath you. The cove with the blowhole is the next cove east, across a rocky shelf strewn with deeply eroded boulders.

There's no better way to discover the blowhole's exact location than to listen for the characteristic *WHOOOOSH!* as it erupts. Once you've found the blowhole, just under ½ mile from the parking area, pick a spot from which to watch it and to enjoy the intricate natural sculptures around this area. It's quite a show!

Return the way you came.

Nakalele blowhole

Fretwork Weathering

Wind is the principal sculptor at Nakalele Point. It's responsible for those elaborately layered and fluted formations around you as you sit watching the blowhole. But other agents are at work, too. Look closely at the faces of the boulders nearby. You'll probably notice on some of their faces a particularly lovely form of weathering: slender partitions of rock separating little hollows, all forming an intricate fretwork. According to *Maui: How It Came To Be*, this elegant "fretwork weathering" is the result of salt spray and of organisms that adhere to the rock, slowly dissolving it away as they grow. Their patient work has left us these treasures of lace in stone.

Fretwork weathering

Trip E1

Waikamoi Ridge

Distance	Elevation gain	Hiking time	Topos
⅓ to 1⅛ miles	100' to 205'	10–30 minutes	*Keanae 7½'* (Optional)

Difficulty: *Easy, tennis shoes recommended*

Highlights: *The Waikamoi Ridge Trail with its two picnic shelters offers you an opportunity to hike without special permission into the rainforest that the Hana Highway "burrows" through. At one time, many of the plants along this trail were identified by signs that are now gone. However, the Division of Forestry and Wildlife hopes to restore the signs soon. Mosquitoes abound here; be sure to bring your jungle juice.*

Driving instructions: From Wailuku, drive east on Highway 32, bearing southeast as it becomes Highway 36 (the Hana Highway). Continue on Highway 36 past the junction with Highway 37 and through Paia. Highway 36 becomes narrow, winding Highway 360 (still the Hana Highway), and all the highway mileage markers are reset to zero at that point. Halfway between the 9-mile and 10-mile markers on Highway 360, pull into and park in a large turnout just below a ridge on the inland side of the highway, 29¼ miles from Wailuku. If the trailhead is unmarked, don't worry: if you were driving toward Hana and just nosed straight into this turnout, your car is probably pointing at the low bank which the trail initially ascends.

Permit/permission required: None.

Description: Leave the parking area going uphill and east on a low bank. You reach a picnic shelter almost immediately, then follow the trail's left fork at the junction just beyond the shelter. You descend a little through huge eucalyptus trees wreathed in giant philodendrons (believe it or not, the philodendrons are just escaped houseplants). Look for the vivid red bracts of lobster-claw heliconia to your right. *Hala*, guava, white ginger, and *ti* line your path here.

At a false fork near a clump of lobster-claw heliconia, keep to the left. Now the trail begins to climb, and you soon reach a junction where the left fork is a spur trail that leads about 10 yards to a bench overlooking the bamboo-clad ridge across from you. (The spur trails aren't on the book's map.) There's a view of the coast to your left here. Back on the main trail, you pass sword fern and sweet fern under *hala* and eucalyptus as, ⅕ mile from the start, the trail begins to level out. A few more steps bring you to a second bench, and the trail soon forks again. You have a choice of making a short loop or a longer out-and-back (optionally picking up the loop as you go back).

The loop takes the righthand fork just beyond the second bench. You descend on a walkway around a densely forested gulch and shortly reach a junction (not shown on the book's map) with a sign that says QUIET TREES AT WORK. The right fork takes you back to the first picnic shelter; the left winds down to the parking lot.

The out-and-back takes the lefthand fork just beyond the second bench and climbs a little past strawberry guava. This section is overgrown, narrow, and slippery, and it has a steep dropoff on the right side. Nearing the ⅓-mile point, the trail levels out, makes a switchback, and climbs a little to a spur trail that goes a few yards to a third bench (the view from this bench is sometimes obscured by dense vegetation). To the right, the main trail goes through hala and swamp mahogany and then bamboo to a junction with an old jeep road. Turn left onto the jeep road to reach the upper picnic shelter, ½ mile from your start. The shelter sits under big mango trees ⅛ mile from this junction. After a rest and a snack here, retrace your steps on the trail you came up on. To pick up the loop, return to the loop-vs.-out-and-back junction and turn left on the loop part described above. Otherwise, continue to retrace your steps to the parking lot.

Lobster-claw heliconia (left) and *koa* (right)

Along the Hana Highway

The "welcome mat" is seldom out for hikers along the Hana Highway. The East Maui Irrigation Company owns much of the land here, and the company does not permit casual hiking on its land. This makes the Waikamoi Ridge Trail especially valuable as an opportunity to explore this rainforest!

Hikes along the Hana Highway

The trip to Hana is much more enjoyable if you spend at least one night in Hana town itself (there are budget accommodations in Hana). This makes it possible for you to drive slowly, stop often, enjoy the sights, and take one or two of these hikes as you go. Trips E1 through E3 are described in terms of driving from Wailuku toward Hana because it makes sense to take those trips in conjunction with your drive to or from Hana town. However, you really need to stay in Hana town in order to have the time to enjoy most of the trips between Trip E4 and Trip E13. Those trips are described as "side trips from Hana town" for that reason.

Yes, you can drive from Wailuku to Hana and back in one long day, but about all you'll have time for is driving, driving, driving!

Trip E2

Keanae Arboretum

Distance	Elevation gain	Hiking time	Topos
1+ mile	70'	½ hour	Keanae 7½' (Optional)

Difficulty: *Easy, tennis shoes recommended*

Highlights: *Keanae Arboretum is a lovely tropical-valley walk you won't want to miss. There's an area of non-native tropical plants, including many ornamental plants you've probably seen but have not been able to identify. There's also an area of native plants, probably including ones you'd hoped to see in the wild but couldn't find or identify. Here, native and non-native plants are identified for you; what an opportunity to learn!*

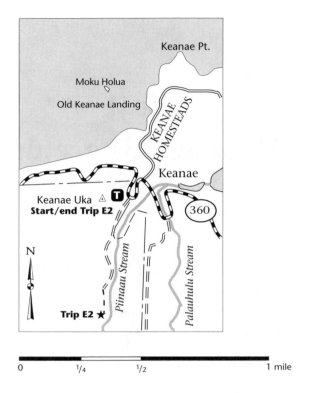

Old Keanae Landing

Moku Holua

Keanae Pt.

KEANAE HOMESTEADS

Keanae

Keanae Uka △ **T**
Start/end Trip E2

360

N

Piinaau Stream

Palauhulu Stream

Trip E2 ★

0   1/4   1/2   1 mile

Driving instructions: Following the driving instructions of Trip E1 past Waikamoi Ridge. Continue east on Highway 360 past Kaumahina State Wayside, where you may want to stop to use the restrooms and to walk up the concrete path to enjoy some good views of the Keanae Peninsula. Around 6 miles past Kaumahina, look for a wide turnout on the inland side of the highway where a fence with a gate marks the boundary of Keanae Arboretum, 35½ miles from Wailuku. Park in this turnout or in another one across the highway.

Permit/permission required: None.

Description: Your hike starts at the gate, through which you pass to walk down an old road under a cover of *hau*, African tulip, and guava. Impatiens blossoms provide vivid spots of white, lipstick pink, and magenta under the dense tree cover. The road curves left to another gate, marking the start of the non-native plant section. Huge clumps of bamboo rise on your left, exotic palm trees on your right. Short side trails branching down to a stream invite you to explore plantings of heliconia, ginger, and other exotics.

A little before the ¼-mile point, you reach the native plant section. Many varieties of hibiscus are represented here. Look for breadfruit trees along the road. You may wonder about their huge, round, pale-green fruits or recall their historical connection to the infamous *Bounty* and Captain Bligh. But surely their most arresting feature is their immense, glossy, deeply lobed leaves.

A feature for which Keanae Arboretum is especially well-known is just ahead of you on this *ti*-lined avenue: many plantings of different kinds of dryland and wetland taro, the latter waving its elongated heart-shaped leaves over a series of gleaming ponds. The rocky road becomes a raised, rocky path as you skirt the taro patches.

Beyond the taro patches, you can follow the path, now a rough and muddy track, upstream past fragrant ginger to a spot where a little cascade spills into a pool shaded by guava and *kukui*. The track becomes little more than a slippery, muddy scramble over tangled roots after this pool, so this is a good place to turn around and return to your car, just over ½ mile from your start.

Breadfruit and Taro

The early Polynesian settlers brought with them to Hawaii a variety of breadfruit (*ulu*) that can be reproduced only from cuttings or shoots (it doesn't produce seeds, though many other varieties do). With only this one variety of breadfruit available in Hawaii, breadfruit was a seasonal rather than a year-round crop. Taro (*kalo*), of which the Hawaiians had many varieties, was a year-round crop in Hawaii, different varieties maturing at different times of the year. In Hawaii, taro became the staple starch. Elsewhere in the Pacific, there were many varieties of breadfruit, bearing fruit at different times of the year, so breadfruit became the staple starch.

Both cooked breadfruit and poi, the edible paste made from taro roots, seem to be foods you have to grow up with in order to enjoy. Try a bag of taro chips (sold alongside potato chips in most Hawaiian markets) even if you can't bring yourself to try *poi*. The chips will grow on you quickly. Don't think about calories as you stare into the empty bag, wondering how they disappeared so fast. Think instead of how you've made a sincere effort to enjoy taro; unlike most who try *poi* for the first time, you've probably succeeded!

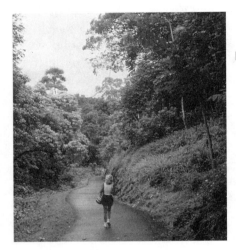

Main path in the Keanae Arboretum

Keanae Arboretum

Trip E3

Puaa Kaa

Distance	Elevation gain	Hiking time	Topos
Negligible	Negligible	Negligible	*Nahiku 7½'* (Optional)

Difficulty: *Very easy, tennis shoes recommended*

Highlights: *Two freshwater pools you can swim in, connected by a small cascade, and three picnic shelters, all in less than 2 minutes' walk from the highway, should tempt you to stay a while at Puaa Kaa. Puaa Kaa gets lots of visitors, but don't let that put you off.*

Driving instructions: Follow the driving instructions of Trips E1 and then E2 past Keanae Arboretum for 2¼ more miles to the parking lot for Puaa Kaa. The parking lot is on the seaward side of the highway,

111

37¾ miles from Wailuku. The pools and picnic shelters are just across the highway from the parking lot.

Permit/permission required: None.

Description: The stream whose bridge you crossed just before you turned into the parking lot at Puaa Kaa divides Puaa Kaa into two sections: a southeast one with access from the southeast side of the stream to two picnic shelters and the upper pool, and a northwest one offering access from the northwest side of the stream to the lower pool and a third picnic shelter.

For the southeast section, you walk up a short rise through strawberry guavas to the first of two small picnic shelters. One picnic shelter is a few steps away, as is the upper pool. You can carefully pick your way across the stream to the other picnic shelter, which is on its west side. (As of this writing, it's easier to get to the west side of the upper pool area from the southeast section.)

There's no easy way from the southeast section to the lower pool, so it's better to return to the highway, cross the bridge, and get to the lower pool by taking the footpath on the northwest side of the bridge.

After your picnic and swim, retrace your steps to your car.

Close-up:
Puaa Kaa
State Park
Not to scale

Trip E4

Ulaino Road

Side Trip from Hana

Distance	Elevation gain	Hiking time	Topos
4 miles	150' (Loss/gain)	2 hours	Hana 7½'

Difficulty: *Moderate, tennis shoes recommended*

Highlights: *The forest that lines this lovely old road includes many exotic flowering species, making it more colorful than other rainforest paths. At the end of the road, there's a cobblestone "beach" and fine coastal scenery. I'll give you some hints about the final highlight but leave you to discover it fully. The road part of this trip is suitable for travel by mountain bicycle as well as by Ankle Express.*

Driving instructions: As I said earlier, I believe that most of the hikes in and around Hana town cannot be enjoyed in conjunction with a one-day trip to and from Hana, so plan to stay in Hana town. This is the first of several such hikes in this book—the side trips from Hana town. I'll give their driving instructions in terms of a reference point in Hana town: Hana Beach County Park, just seaward of the intersection of Ua Kea Road and Keawa Place in Hana. But first, you need to get to Hana town....

To get to Hana town and Hana Beach County Park: It's 54 miles from Wailuku to Hana town. To get to Hana Beach County Park, stay on Highway 360 past Puaa Kaa and the turnoffs to Hana Airport and Waianapanapa State Park. The highway forks just past the Hana Medical Center; the left fork is Ua Kea Road. Bear left on it and drive past the Hana Cultural Center to meet Keawa Place just where you can look left down to Hana Bay and Hana Beach County Park. Turn left

Beach at the end of Ulaino Road

and drive a short block down to the parking lot for the park. It's a convenient place to stop, relax, enjoy the view, and orient yourself to Hana town. When you've got your bearings, drive to wherever you're staying in Hana, note the distance, and adjust the driving distances given in this trip and Trips E5 through E13 accordingly. You probably won't need to drive at all to get to the start of Trip E10.

To get to the start of this side trip: From Hana Beach County Park, drive back on Ua Kea Road north past the Hana Medical Center, then north and west past the turnoffs to Waianapanapa State Park and Hana Airport. One mile west of the turnoff to Waianapanapa State Park, turn right (seaward) onto Ulaino Road. A sign on the highway directs you to Kahanu Gardens, which is down Ulaino Road. Drive down Ulaino Road to the end of the pavement, ¾ mile from the highway and 4¼ miles from Hana Beach County Park. Park off the road here where you won't block gates or driveways. (Yes, you could drive down Ulaino Road. But it is so delightful to walk on, and it soon becomes so rough and potholed, that you'll want to start your hike here.)

Permit/permission required: None.

Description: Be alert when walking on a road! In general, I recommend that when you are walking on a road, you assume that anyone operating a vehicle on that road is deaf, blind, and insane.

Follow the road generally northwest, initially along open pastures bordered by guava and *kukui*. In the deep grass bordering the road, you're likely to see the small, orange-y flowers of an upright *ilima*, the blue spikes of cayenne vervain, and the pink-and-orange flowerheads of lantana. Planes from nearby Hana Airport buzz overhead occasionally. As you near the ½-mile point, a row of tall *hau* trees brackets a cattle guard. You cross the cattle guard and soon ford a stream under huge mango trees just before reaching the gate of Kahanu Gardens (on your right, seaward). Look for dwarf poinciana trees, stunning in their brilliant red-and-yellow blossoms, across the road from the gate.

A little beyond ¾ mile, Ulaino Road passes through a magnificent forest of *kukui* and *hala* trees, punctuated by an occasional mango tree. There is a lush understory of ferns, and ephiphytic ferns grow high in the trees. As the forest opens up around 1¾ miles, you pass some homes and ford a charming stream with several small cascades. The yards around the homes present a colorful display of ornamental ginger, variegated *ti*, heliconia, impatiens, and many other exotic plants. The road forks at a planting of the very symmetical Norfolk pine; take the left fork here.

Almost 2 miles from your start, the road dips down to a stream that's pooled behind a cobblestone barrier near its mouth. Across the pool, a cliff of black rock forms a wall almost hidden in the rich green of overhanging *kukui* trees. Deep in amongst the leaves you may

Palapalai fern (left), *ie'ie* (right)

Painiu with yellow-orange berries (left), *ohe naupaka* (right)

glimpse seep springs feeding the pool. Turn seaward on the cobble-stones and continue on the cobbles across the stream's mouth. The black lavas of the coastal cliffs, the intense blue of the turbulent sea, the mirror-like pool, and the vivid green of the coastal rainforest make an unforgettable picture.

Standing near the cobblestone barrier across the stream's mouth, look northwest across the stream and up the coast about 200 yards for the final highlight of this hike. Do you see it—the water falling over the cliff and down to the rocky beach? If tide and surf permit, you can pick your way across the barrier to explore this waterfall and what's at its base! (This last segment is up to you; the route shown on the book's map is just an approximation.)

When you can bear to tear yourself away from here, return the way you came.

Kahanu Gardens

Kahanu Gardens, a branch of the National Tropical Botanical Gardens, is home to Pi'ilanihale *Heiau*, thought to be one of the largest temples in Hawaii. Self-guided tours will take you through exhibits of native plants, Polynesian-introduced plants and a modern collection. Open Monday through Friday, from 10 A.M.-2 P.M. (closed on some holidays). $5/adults; 12 and under are free. (808) 248-8912.

Trip E5

Waianapanapa Cave
Side Trip from Hana

Distance	Elevation gain	Hiking time	Topos
⅓ mile	Negligible	Less than 10 minutes	*Hana 7½'*

Difficulty: *Very easy, tennis shoes recommended*

Highlights: *This very short loop trip offers a chance to look into a cave whose floor is a pool of water and which figures in a famous and tragic legend (below).*

Driving instructions: From Hana Beach County Park, drive back on Ua Kea Road north past the Hana Medical Center 2½ miles to the marked turnoff for Waianapanapa State Park, on your right. Follow this

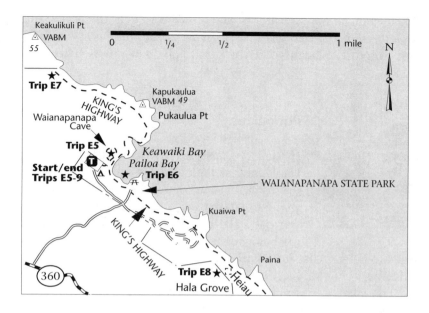

one-lane road ½ mile seaward to the park, then turn left and follow a very potholed road a little less than ¼ mile more past the tent-camping area to a parking lot, just under 3¼ miles total. All Waianapanapa State Park trips in this book (E5 through E9) start from this area.

Permit/permission required: None.

Description: A sign on the seaward edge of the parking lot points left (north) to the cave. You descend a paved trail and stairs under dense *hau* to the first of two fern-draped openings into the cave. The pool you see through this opening is sometimes reddish-colored from the millions of tiny shrimp that live in it. Continue ahead along the impatiens- and ginger-lined path, ascending some stairs, to a short spur path leading to a second cave opening. Walk the few steps down the spur to get a better look through this opening. The cave is said to have a second, dry chamber reachable only by swimming across the pool, as Popoalaea and her attendant did (below).

Now, back on the main path, ascend the next set of stairs past ferns, ginger, and *ti*. The path soon curves back to the parking lot, passing a sign with the cave's legend on it (see also below). You *could* leave

Waianapanapa now, but I hope you'll stay to walk to the nearby over-look to enjoy the view of Waianapanapa's beautiful black-sand beach and sculptured sea cliffs—maybe even to take some more hikes!

Popoalaea

As related by Martha Beckwith in her classic *Hawaiian Mythology*, the chief Kaakea received the Hana chiefess Popoalaea as his wife as a reward for his victory in a series of games that tested his strength. Kaakea was a very jealous man, and he was particularly jealous of Popoalaea's fondness for her younger brother. Hence, he was all too ready to believe false rumors about her infidelity, and he began sharp-ening his axe to kill her.

Popoalaea fled with her attendant, took refuge in the dry cavern at Waianapanapa above the pool of water, and secretively visited a near-by village at night for food. Unfortunately, the villagers reported the mysterious visitors to Kaakea. Their exact hiding place was not easy to find, but one day Kaakea saw on the water of the pool the shadow of the fly whisk the attendant was waving for her mistress. (Some sources say it was the reflection of Popoalaea's *kahili*, the feather-crowned stan-dard of the *alii*, that Kaakea saw.) Kaakea seized and murdered both women.

It's said that when the water in the pool turns reddish, it's red with Popoalaea's blood. Each morning, it's also said, rainbow colors (*anapa*) play over the pool as a sign of Popoalaea's innocence. What a sad fate, but what a beautiful spot in which to be remembered.

Trip E6

Waianapanapa Black-Sand Beach

Side Trip from Hana

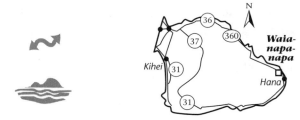

Distance	Elevation gain	Hiking time	Topos
⅒ mile	40' (Loss/gain)	Less than 5 minutes	*Hana 7½'* (Optional)

Difficulty: *Very easy, tennis shoes recommended*

Highlights: *If you've been astonished at the beauty of Maui's many white-sand beaches, just wait till you see this gorgeous black-sand beach! A fair number of the people who gaze longingly at Waianapanapa's black-sand beach from the overlook near the parking lot seem unable to find their way down to it. Here's how to get to it.*

Driving instructions: Follow the driving instructions of Trip E5.

Permit/permission required: None.

Description: From the seaward end of the parking lot, where the sign directs you left to the caves (Trip E5), turn right and head generally south on the path. Pause at the overlook of the black-sand beach to take in this glorious view. Among other lovely features, you'll count at least two natural arches in the cliffs cupping the beach. A few steps farther on, the path forks. The left fork here leads steeply down to the southeast end of the black-sand beach, which curves northwest away from the base of the path.

If you find the black-sand beach too crowded for your taste, there's a little black-*cobble* cove farther on. (The distance, elevation gain, and time given above don't include the jaunt to this cove.) Walk to the far end of the black-sand beach (away from the path you came down on). Here you'll find a little trail through the beach *naupaka*. Follow it upward through *hau*, *noni*, pink-flowered clover with sticky seeds, and sweet fern. After a brief level stretch, the trail descends to the black-cobble cove. **Caution:** swimming at Waianapanapa can be dangerous because of strong currents and high surf.

When you're ready, return the way you came.

Waianapanapa

Black-sand Beaches

Black-sand beaches are rare anywhere in the world. Most beaches are of light-colored sand. In the tropics, that usually means that the sand is pulverized coral—a gift of the sea. Black-sand beaches are a gift of the land. Some form when hot lava flows enter the ocean, causing a steam explosion that blows the molten material into millions of glassy fragments. You'll find a very few beaches like that on the Big Island of Hawaii; walking on their coarse sand is like walking on tiny beads of jet. These beaches are short-lived, as there's no reliable source of new material to replace what the ocean and the wind carry away. The fragments are the result of a single steam explosion. The chances of another flow occurring in the exactly the same place and in the same way, yielding similar fragments to replenish the beach, are very remote. The once-famous black-sand beach at Kalapana on the Big Island is all but gone now, its glassy sands swept away or blown inland. (It also suffered major damage

Waianapanapa

when its section of coast abruptly sank about 3 feet in the powerful earthquake of November 1975.)

Other black-sand beaches are the products of erosion—particles of dark-colored material weathered from the rocks at the ocean's edge. That's the source of this black-sand beach here at Waianapanapa and at a few other sites in the Hawaiian Islands. The patient work of erosion has created not only those lovely arches and sea stacks from the surrounding black cliffs but also this beautiful little beach. As you can see, there's plenty of material left to erode, so *this* black-sand beach will be here for a little while.

Trip E7

King's Highway (North)
Side Trip from Hana

Distance	Elevation gain	Hiking time	Topos
2⅔ miles	160'	1⅓ hours	*Hana 7½'*

Difficulty: *Strenuous due to very rough terrain; hiking boots strongly recommended*

Highlights: *Scenery—the dramatic coastal scenery of the cliffs around Waianapanapa State Park and the sweeping views inland up the slopes of Haleakala. On your way, you visit the black-sand beach and black-cobble cove.*

Driving instructions: Follow the driving instructions of Trip E5.

Permit/permission required: None.

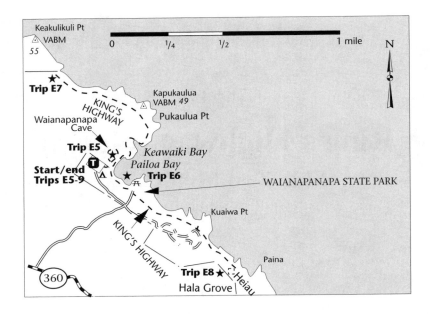

Description: Follow Trip E6 down to the black-sand beach and over to the black-cobble cove. Cross the black-cobble cove and follow the trail as it climbs again, toward *hala* trees and past a stone structure. With the help of a switchback, you're soon atop the cliffs in a region of twisted *aa* lava. The trail bears northeast through more *hala* and beach *naupaka* and follows the coast, passing high above bouldery Keawaiki Bay, where the waves surge in too forcefully for swimming. You pass through a forest of *hala* and find yourself in an open wilderness of *aa* lava, a landscape characteristic of the remaining coastal segments of the King's Highway (see below).

In ½ mile you reach a junction where you turn left (northwest); the right fork leads out to the remains of Kapukaulua VABM. If you pause for any length of time on this trail, you're apt to find your boots covered with a kind of ant that seems determined to conduct mass explorations of any stationary object. The rocks may be swarming with them, so keep your stops brief.

You pass a small shrine and continue through the *aa*. The trail dips into a deep gully where, offshore, remnants of the sea cliff stand isolated, washed in turquoise water and white foam. You come out of one

Hala fruit

Hala tree with distinctive stiltlike roots

gully to descend into another. On the other side of the second gully, the trail may be quite faint. A little exploring will soon reveal the trail, and you follow it—very rough now—to a cove whose beach consists of large, rounded cobbles. Pick your way across the cove on the cobbles, then climb back up to the cliffs on a steep, very loose track.

You presently climb a little, pass a narrow natural arch, and reach an anticlimactic end, probably signaled by the wind sock, at Hana Airport, 1⅓ miles from your start. It's time to turn around and retrace your steps.

The King's Highway

A remnant of old Hawaii, the King's Highway is a trail around Maui established in prehistoric times for the king of Maui and his messengers and partly rebuilt in historic times. It's also called the *alaloa* or the Hono a Piilani Highway. Martha Foss Fleming, in *Old Trails of Maui*, estimated its original length at roughly 138 miles. Today, the hikable fragments are those that pass through *aa* fields here at Waianapanapa and east of La Pérouse Bay. Passage over the *aa* would have been very difficult if this trail had not been especially constructed. On easier terrain, the trail followed natural routes like beaches, and it has disappeared because there was never a *built-up* trail. Elsewhere, it's disappeared on account of erosion and neglect or been buried under newer construction.

Any lava field holds surprises no traveler needs. Fragile lava formations, such as thin ceilings over hidden lava tubes, can crumble underfoot, leaving you hanging in midair or, worse, falling. The King's Highway provides a safe passage through lava fields. The prehistoric Hawaiians invested a great deal of time and labor in building this roadway over the impossible jumble of the *aa* wilderness. As you'll find when you hike them, the waterless, shadeless *aa* fields can be brutally hot in the fiery sun. Imagine working to build the King's Highway in that heat, lifting and carrying the stones, placing them, and keeping the trailbed relatively level for all those miles.

These segments of the King's Highway can be demanding, for the *aa* rocks on the trailbed are loose and sharp. They roll around under your boots and make each step a little more work than you're used to. The trail makes no concession to the terrain. It simply marches as straight as it can steeply up, across, and steeply down the lava ridges and gullies. But look around you: what more could be done in this *aa* field without destroying it completely? Well done, I say!

Trip E8

Ohala *Heiau*

Side Trip from Hana

Distance	Elevation gain	Hiking time	Topos
1½ miles	Negligible	¾ hour	Hana 7½'

Difficulty: *Easy, hiking boots strongly recommended*

Highlights: *Magnificent scenery as in Trip E7; the coastal scenery is perhaps even better on this trip. Your visit includes the well-known hala groves of Waianapanapa, a fine, noisy blowhole, and a heiau, too.*

Driving instructions: Follow the driving instructions of Trip E5.

Permit/permission required: None.

Blowhole

Description: Follow Trip E6 from the parking lot to the point where the trail to the black-sand beach forks left. Take the right fork here, quickly passing the tent campground and then a cemetery in the shade of tropical almond trees, to yet another fork. Go left at this fork, and you'll soon reach some picnic tables. This is a good place to pause to enjoy the view: the fresh tropical green of Haleakala's slopes, the black of Waianapanapa's basalt cliffs, and the foam-streaked blue-green of the sea. Notice the column-like formations in the cliffs; you'll see formations like these often along this coastal walk.

Now you descend a little as the trail winds past *aa* flows and through beach *naupaka* and morning glory. Dense groves of *hala* trees rise just inland of the path; often, the path is plentifully strewn with their long, sawtoothed, pointed leaves and their chunky orange fruit. Use trails and even old roads strike off into the *hala* groves, but you stay on the coastal trail. Between ⅓ and ¼ mile, listen for the roar of a big blowhole that's just seaward off the trail. When it actually "blows" depends on tide and surf (some wave combinations aren't strong enough to make it erupt), and it may take you by surprise. Look for low-lying strands of *akulikuli* in the rocks along your path here.

Near ⅔ mile, you cross a cement-reinforced bridge. Soon after that, you descend steeply. At the bottom of this descent, crudely hacked into the cliff, the path continues over a lava shelf and along the crumbling cliffs. At ¾ mile, you reach signed OHALA HEIAU, a raised platform of black boulders. It's a picturesque spot, and you'll want to spend some time here. Don't climb on the *heiau* or its walls. The lava field may be swarming with busy ants, so be prepared to defend your lunch.

When you're ready, retrace your steps from here. Or, if you feel the urge to go farther, continue toward Kainalimu Bay as described in the next trip.

Heiaus, graves, and shrines

These rugged and beautiful cliffs hold many sites of religious significance. Besides the _heiau_ and the numerous small shrines, there are mounds of _aa_ that may be ancient, raised graves. While it's a custom elsewhere to leave leaf-wrapped rocks as an offering at these shrines and _heiaus_, signs here ask you not to disturb the site by moving, removing, or wrapping any rocks.

There's a sense of the supernatural here in the presence of so much natural beauty; perhaps the sounds of wind and waves carry echoes of ancient prayers chanted at these solemn places. Please treat all _heiaus_, graves, shrines, and any offerings left at them with respect.

The "trail" beyond Ohala _heiau_ that formerly went to Kainalimu Bay has deteriorated so badly that it's not worth your trouble. Furthermore, someone has built an eyesore of a fishing camp right in its path, pushing a 4WD road down to it. Ugh!

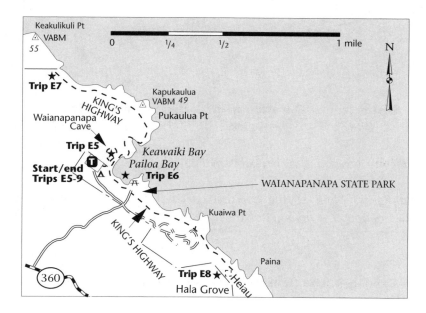

Trip E9

King's Highway S
to Ka: Bay
from Hana

TRAIL CLOSED INDEFINITELY

Distance	Elevation gain	Hiking time	Topos
5 miles	Negligible	2½ hours	Hana 7½'

Difficulty: Strenuous, hiking boots mandatory

Highlights: More of the spectacular coastal scenery that makes Waianapanapa so unforgettable.

Driving instructions: Follow the driving instructions of Trip E5.

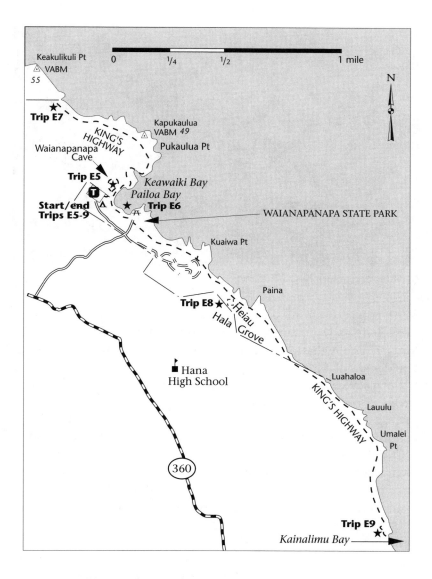

Permit/permission required: None.

Description: Follow Trip E8 to the *heiau*. A low rock wall stretching seaward from the *hala* grove keeps you away from the *heiau* proper. To continue your hike, pass through an opening in the wall near the wall's seaward end. A few yards beyond the *heiau*, a fence runs inland, perpendicular to the coast, and the King's Highway passes through it. Beyond this point, the King's Highway becomes rougher and fainter. At

Cobblestones mark King's Highway

some points, you'll have to hunt around for it; please be careful in these sharp and sometimes unstable lava boulders. A telltale sign of the King's Highway that's particularly evident and useful here is a smooth boulder laid flat in the *aa* trailbed.

At a stretch of coast just over 1 mile from your start, look for a long sweep of coastal cliffs where the basalt columns are especially well-shaped, looking almost manmade-more about this below. Nearly 1⅓ miles from your start, you cross the end of a road that heads inland to your right; you continue along the King's Highway, which becomes even rougher now. The *aa*'s basic gray-black color is varied here and there by bands of red and brown and by whitish lichens, and the *aa* plain is broken by bizarre lava spires twisting skyward. Small ironwood trees grow here, their green foliage incongruously feathery and fresh against the dark, desolate lava.

Presently you cross a large field of smooth *pahoehoe* lava pocked by broken lava tubes and caves and invaded by beach *naupaka*. Here, you must follow ducks (small piles of rocks obviously set up by people) as the King's Highway is very indistinct. Don't follow them blindly, though; test your next foothold to be sure it's sound and will support you.

Nearing the 2½-mile point, you pass a sign that says WAIANAPANAPA STATE PARK 3 MILES (it isn't that far). The track soon dips into a buggy, tree-filled gully, where you may want a spider stick to get past some hiker-size webs and their occupants. The track bears left at the bottom of the gully and debouches at the cobblestone beach of Kainalimu Bay. Rest here, enjoy this wild, lonely bay, and then turn around and retrace your steps to your car.

Basalt Columns

When a lava flow forms a pond that cools slowly, it may crack into column-like shapes like those you see here along the Waianapanapa coast. Cooling lava shrinks, and cracks form as sections of rock shrink apart. These cracks tend to go from the top to the bottom of the cooling mass, producing the basic "column" effect. The cracks intersect, and columns with from three to eight sides form in the cooling mass. As every honeybee knows, a six-sided structure is the most efficient, and six-sided columns tend to predominate. A columnar formation is a spectacular sight when it's exposed to view. Columnar formations are said to be rare on Hawaii, so it's a special pleasure to see them here. (On the mainland, Devils Postpile National Monument in California's Sierra Nevada includes one of the better-known large columnar formations.)

Along the trail at *Waianapanapa*

Trip E10

Hana Bay

Side Trip from Hana

Distance	Elevation gain	Hiking time	Topos
⅔ mile	Negligible	10 minutes	*Hana 7½'*

Difficulty: *Very easy, tennis shoes recommended*

Highlights: *A morning walk around Hana Bay offers fine views of Hana from the wharf.*

Driving instructions: This hike begins at Hana Beach County Park (see Trip E4).

Permit/permission required: None.

N

Hana Medical
⊕ Center
125

Ua Kea Rd

360

△ VABM 545

Puu o Kahaula

Nanualele
Pt

HANA BAY

Hana Beach County Park

Light

Start/end ★
Trip E10
🅣

Keawa Pl

Hana

Kauiki Head

0   ¹/₄   ¹/₂   1 mile

Description: Hana town is lovely, but it can get quite hot and humid. A long walk around Hana can be almost as debilitating as a walk through a steambath with hills. Add to this no sidewalks and streets with fast traffic that may come popping unexpectedly over the top of the hill you're walking on. I recommend that you keep your strolls in Hana town short, and restrict them to the early morning hours. With that caution, it's time to see Hana Bay.

Whatever direction you're facing when you get out of your car, it's hard to miss the prominent hill on the south side of Hana Bay, Kauiki (ka-oo-EE-kee) Head. Walk around the bay as it curves toward Kauiki Head. Follow the paved road as it bears left at the base of Kauiki Head at a little parking lot and out onto the wharf to take in a wonderful view of Hana town and its surroundings. A line of green-clad cinder cones marks one of Haleakala's rift zones. Nearer the town, a gray cross on sensuously shaped Puu o Kahaula honors the memory of Paul Fagan. When sugar production declined here and Hana's economy faltered in the 1940s, Paul Fagan helped revive Hana by introducing cattle ranching (Hana Ranch) and tourism (Hotel Hana-Maui). Grazing cattle dot the hillsides above the town now. And just in front of you, the blue waters of Hana Bay lap at the wharf.

Hana was one of the favorite places of the *alii*. Hana had everything, especially plenty to eat with little effort required to get food. The community maintained a lookout on Kauiki Head for schools of fish. Before Europeans came to Hawaii, Kauiki Head was covered with a native bunchgrass and could be climbed. Now, it's almost impossible to climb because of its dense cover of exotic plants. It's reported that the few who climb it get no reward for their effort: ironwoods block the view from its top.

Kauiki Head was used as a fortress; not surprisingly, it was the site of many battles. Hana is worth fighting over, and this isolated corner of East Maui has often been ruled by the Big Island of Hawaii. In 1754, the king of Hawaii conquered East Maui Kahekili, then king of Maui, recaptured East Maui in 1775. The fortress at Kauiki Head did not fall in battle. Instead, Kahekili had to cut off the water supply to the fortress. When the fortress surrendered, Kahekili showed his contempt for the defenders by baking their bodies in earthen ovens.

As you'd expect, Kauiki Head also has its share of legends. One legend about the demigod Maui relates that long ago, the sky was so low

Hana Bay

Hotel Hana Maui

that people couldn't stand straight. They even had to walk bent over. From the top of Kauiki Head, Maui pushed the sky up so that people could walk and stand upright.

Back at the little parking lot at the base of the wharf and of Kauiki Head, you may notice a rough use trail that heads seaward (left) from here out onto Kauiki Head, but don't take it. The trail used to lead to a plaque marking Queen Kaahumanu's birthplace, but the trail has been erased by a landslide. I recommend you not try to cross the slope, as it seems ready to give way again. It's unfortunate that you can't go out to pay your respects to Queen Kaahumanu any more because, as outlined in "Geology and History, Natural and Human" in this book, she became Kamehameha's favorite wife. After his death she was a leader in overthrowing the *kapu* that had been the basis of Hawaiian social structure. Here's something to think about: how would Hawaii's history have been different if the *kapu* been in force when the first missionaries arrived?

After having pondered that question, retrace your steps to your car.

Trip E11

Oheo Gulch Pools
(Kuloa Loop)
Side Trip from Hana

Distance	Elevation gain	Hiking time	Topos
Just under ⅔ mile	120' (Loss/gain)	20 minutes	Kipahulu 7½' (Optional)

Difficulty: *Very easy, tennis shoes recommended*

Highlights: *A splash in Oheo Stream's famous pools is what most people come here for. This is the area that was once erroneously referred to as the Seven Sacred Pools. In fact, there are more than seven pools, and there's no evidence that they were ever considered sacred. But there's more to enjoy than the pools: Don't overlook the marvelous coastal views* here. You can often see the Big Island of Hawaii across Alenuihaha Channel. For the latest information on the Oheo Gulch area, call the Kipahulu Ranger Station at (808) 248-7375.

Driving instructions: From the intersection of Ua Kea Road and Keawa Place in Hana, drive uphill on Keawa Place and turn left onto the Hana Highway. From here, it's 10⅓ miles to the Kipahulu section of Haleakala National Park, which is where Oheo Stream is. At 7⅓ miles from Hana, you cross a bridge just inland of which beautiful Wailua Falls drops into a fine pool. You may be tempted to pull over onto the shoulder and walk back for a dip. On the road, you reach the park boundary, cross Oheo Stream, and follow signs a short distance to a dirt parking lot on the seaward side. In spite of its remoteness, enough people find their way to the Kipahulu section to fill this little parking lot to overflowing by midday. There are restrooms here but *no drinking water*. You must either purify any water you get from the stream or bring your own drinking water with you.

Permit/permission required: None, but pay your fee or show your pass at the ranger station.

Description: The marked trail to the lower pools begins at the northeast edge of the parking lot. Head downhill (east) toward the sea on a paved path, toward the ranger station and an information sign. You soon reach a junction (not on the map) where it's right to the ranger station and left to continue to the pools. The ranger station has interesting interpretive displays as well as books and maps. At the junction with the trail to Makahiku and Waimoku falls—the Pipiwai Trail, which branches left—go right to the pools on the Kuloa Point trail. (This is the junction that's about ½ inch west of and slightly down from the star that marks the goal of this trip.) Continuing to the pools, you stay on the wide, main trail, ignoring use trails that branch off. You pass Java plum and *kukui* trees, then cross a meadow dotted with clumps of *hala*. Soon you're on a bluff overlooking the ocean, next to the stone ruins of an old Hawaiian community. There are beautiful views up and down the coast and across Alenuihaha Channel south-southeast to the Big Island. Pause to enjoy the interpretive displays.

Now the trail curves left (north-northeast) toward the stream, and it's just a minute or so before you hear the sounds of merriment from the

141

the pools. At the next trail junction, just over ⅓ mile from the parking lot, the right fork is a spur trail leading to views of the coast and, uphill, of Oheo Gulch. You take the left fork, and another trail junction pops up almost immediately. The right fork here will take you down steep stairs to the lowest pool. From there, you can work your way upstream to the other pools (not part of this hike). The pools are generally quite crowded.

Oheo Gulch

The left fork (that is, continuing on the main trail) takes you uphill to an area where railings allow you to safely enjoy the view over the stream and snap some photos. *Hala, ti,* and sisal clothe the steep slope below your viewpoint. Continuing, you presently curve away from the stream under tropical almond trees, almost reaching the road. You could close this loop on the road, but it's nicer to turn left and take the trail, now on stairs for a short stretch, back to the parking lot. You pass a junction where you continue ahead (the left fork goes back to the stone ruins you visited earlier on this hike).

At ½ mile you reach another trail junction (it's the first one you passed at the beginning of this hike). Here, you turn continue ahead and soon reach the parking lot, a little less than ⅔ mile from your start.

While Paddling in the Pools . . .

Keep an eye out for the water level. If it rises suddenly, that may indicate that a flash flood is imminent. Get out of the water immediately! You don't want to be swept downstream and drowned, much less be swept out to sea. It's said that the gray sharks around the mouth of Oheo Stream have acquired a taste for human flesh—a heck of a way to end your Maui vacation! But maybe sloshing around in the pools isn't all you're here for. You'd like to see some waterfalls! Read on—Trips E12 and E13 take you to splendid Makahiku Falls and then to enchanting Waimoku Falls.

143

Trip E12

Makahiku Falls
Side Trip from Hana

Distance	Elevation gain	Hiking time	Topos
⅔ mile	250′	20 minutes	Kipahulu 7½′

Difficulty: *Easy, tennis shoes recommended*

Highlights: *An easy hike through the lovely hills and pastures upslope of the highway brings you to an overlook of spectacular Makahiku Falls. You can swim off the dust of the hike in the fine pools behind the falls. Note that it's possible for both falls, Makahiku and Waimoku, to be almost dry if there's been a drought. But you'll enjoy this hike even if the falls are barely dribbling.*

View of dry Oheo Gulch/stream

Driving instructions: Follow the driving instructions of Trip E11.

Permit/permission required: None.

Description: You could head seaward toward the pools east of the highway and pick up the trail to Makahiku and Waimoku falls from that route (Trip E11). But there's a shorter route: From the parking lot, face the entrance to orient yourself and then go right, roughly parallel to and on the seaward side of the parking lot wall, to pick up a path that in a few yards leads you to a pedestrian crossing of the highway. Cross the highway and curve right to pick up the official trail, paralleling the highway briefly. (If coming from the pools, at a T-junction, go right.)

The trail shortly leads uphill under Java plum and on rocky footing to reach the edge of Oheo Gulch. The trail then bears left (west) along the south side of the gulch and climbs moderately through a dense forest of Christmas berry and strawberry guava. Many use trails branch off this main trail toward the rim of the gulch; keep your eyes peeled so you can stick to the main trail. The trail may be hard to follow at times, and you'll be thankful for the TRAIL signs the Park Service has posted here and there. You presently leave the forest for a track through an open stand of guava and Christmas berry, where there may be good guava-hunting—but watch your step as you thrash through deep weeds and across uneven ground.

You soon see a stone wall to your right, on the rim of Oheo Gulch. Sites along this wall provide excellent views of Makahiku Falls. This is a good vantage point for a photo of the falls, too. Look for white-tailed tropicbirds soaring over the chasm. When you're ready, return the way you came.

Kipahulu Valley

You've been hiking in lower Kipahulu Valley on this trail. If you look at a topographic map of Maui, the immense Keanae and Kaupo valleys will probably catch your eye. You can see how they meet atop Haleakala to form Haleakala Crater. Now look to the east of Kaupo Valley, and you'll notice the deep "scoop" of Kipahulu Valley.

Kipahulu Valley is the result of distinct episodes of volcanism and stream-cutting. The first episode of volcanism built Haleakala. A second episode of volcanism covered the original volcano with new lavas. Rain soon sent streams radiating from the top of the shield volcano, cutting into it as they flowed. At Kipahulu, a stream carved a huge valley much deeper than the present one, cutting through both the newer and the older lavas. The next episode of volcanism sent new lava flowing down the huge valley, nearly filling it. A stream soon began cutting through the newest lava. Before this second stream could re-create the original valley by erosion, still more lava flowed from Haleakala, partly filling the newer valley. Now the present-day Palikea Stream, the western tributary of Oheo Stream, is scooping out the present Kipahulu Valley, while Pipiwai Stream, the eastern tributary of Oheo Stream, is scooping out a smaller side valley.

It seems likely that Palikea Stream will continue eroding Kipahulu Valley's headwall back toward Kaupo Valley and breach that wall, just as the streams forming Kaupo and Keanae valleys once breached their headwalls to create the crater—unless Haleakala erupts and fills Kipahulu again. In the meantime, a dense rainforest fills upper Kipahulu Valley, and many rare species of birds and plants flourish only there. Upper Kipahulu Valley is a scientific reserve closed to the public so that it can be protected, preserved, and studied.

The dense growth of the upper valley soaks up the abundant rain, releasing it in streams and springs and ensuring a good water supply for the settled areas below. The lands of Kipahulu are very productive. They once supported a large population and were, like Hana, fought over by the *alii*. Kipahulu was gradually abandoned as the center of commerce on Maui shifted to Lahaina in the early nineteenth century.

Trip E13

Waimoku Falls
Side Trip from Hana

Distance	Elevation gain	Hiking time	Topos
Just under 4 miles	560'	Just under 2 hours	Kipahulu 7½'

Difficulty: *Moderate, hiking boots strongly recommended*

Highlights: *After your visit to Makahiku Falls, you continue uphill to Waimoku Falls. Along the way, you pass through stands of giant bamboo so dense that what little light filters down to you seems tinted green. Waimoku Falls is lovely, but the pool at its base is too shallow to swim in, and the danger of rockfall is great.*

Driving instructions: Follow the driving instructions of Trip E11.
Permit/permission required: None.

Description: Follow Trip E12 to Makahiku Falls. Continuing, you soon pass through a fence (please close the gate) and bear north past some banyan trees. Your progress between here and the 1-mile point is apt to be slower than usual if you like guavas, for trees bearing abundant fruit line this stretch.

Nearing the 1-mile point, you cross an open area and descend slightly into a dense growth of guavas. Whatever the other hazards may be here, you're in very real danger of getting beaned by falling guavas. Mosquitoes are sure to be a problem from here on, if they haven't been already, so apply that jungle juice now.

In a few more steps, you reach and cross Palikea Stream (a tributary of Oheo Stream) on a footbridge and, bearing left to pick up the trail on the other side, cross another footbridge, and scramble up very steeply under guavas and mangoes, negotiating a few short switchbacks. Soon you're walking between walls of giant bamboo. Wooden walkways help you across boggy spots in and between these bamboo forests; watch out for missing planks.

The dense bamboo forest, formerly broken, is now continuous, the route seeming to have just been hacked through the giant stalks. As you grope through the twilight of the dense stand, a breeze may rattle the stalks, playing random percussion music on them, and rustle the leaves, making a thin accompaniment with their whisperings.

Beyond the bamboo at last, you cross a streamlet (watch the poor footing). In a few more yards, the trail becomes less distinct as you cross several channels of Pipiwai Stream flowing from Waimoku Falls, which you can see just ahead. Follow the trail or the channels a few more steps almost to the shallow pool at the waterfall's base, almost 2 miles from your start. Note and heed the warning signs here. Waimoku Falls is cradled in a deep little amphitheater with sheer walls to which cling mosses and ferns. Its base is surrounded by shattered rock; there's a real danger of rockfall here. The principal cascade is on the left side, but smaller cascades slip down the walls on every side. Bands of solid lava rock alternate with looser bands of consolidated ash or clinker, layer upon layer up the amphitheater walls. Spray from the waterfall cools and dampens everything.

Rest awhile and enjoy this lovely sight. When you're ready, return the way you came.

Waimoku Falls

Waterfalls at Work

In Hawaii, the terrain tends to consist of alternating layers of resistant lava and less resistant material, such as consolidated ash or clinker. The layers you see alternating in the amphitheater walls at Waimoku Falls are an example. A stream wears through the softer layer faster and cascades over the remaining harder layer. The force of the falling water wears away the rock at the base of the falls, forming a pool. Undercut by that process, rock above the pool succumbs to gravity and falls away, shattering at the base of the falls. This process wears the stream's channel farther and farther back into the slope. Over eons, the stream cuts its gorge back toward its headwaters. Because harder and softer layers alternate, many streams form a chain of waterfalls on their long descent to the sea. A waterfall like Waimoku may be—and in this case *is*—just one in the chain.

Trip E14

Kaupo to
Haleakala Park Boundary

Distance	Elevation gain	Hiking time	Topos
6½ miles	2730'	3¼ hours	Kaupo 7½'

Difficulty: Strenuous, hiking boots strongly recommended

Alert: This is a very stiff hike. Take plenty of water and choose a cool, even overcast, day for this trip.

Highlights: The sweeping views down Haleakala's southern slopes from this steep, breezy, very strenuous trail defy words. The scene upslope to Kaupo Gap's mountain-guarded portals is just as stunning. A few miles east, scores of people crowd into the Kipahulu District parking lot to visit the pools and waterfalls of Oheo Gulch. But here at remote Kaupo, where *there are no typical tourist attractions, you'll probably have the trail all to yourself.*

Driving instructions: You can't get to Kaupo from Kipahulu in the average rental car. As mentioned earlier, much of the road between Kaupo and Kipahulu is unpaved and extremely rough. It's subject to washouts, landslides, and closures. If you must take it, check with the highway department first to see if it's open. If it's open, then tackle it only in a high-clearance 4WD vehicle with plenty of gas and well-stocked with food and water.

There's no gas until distant Keokea, but you can get food and drink at the Kaupo Store at Kaupo. The store is open Monday through Friday from about 9:30 A.M. to 5:30 P.M. and stocks cold drinks, snacks, and other simple supplies—cash only. The store also has a restroom. It's a family venture, the owners are delightful people, and a visit to the Kaupo Store is not to be missed. Call ahead to verify the hours (808) 248-8054).

Kaupo Gap

HALEAKALA
NATIONAL PARK

N

WT ● ☆ **Trips E14 and H7**

KIPAHULU

FOREST

RESERVE

Healani Stream

KAUPO
TRAIL

● Water Tank

N

KAUPO TRAIL

BM ╳
1576

Kahualau Gulch

Opakalua Gulch

Keaku Valley

Kaokao Ridge

WT ●
Corral

● Water Tanks

Segment
approximated

🄣
**Start/end
Trip E14**

to Hwy. 31,
Kaupo Store

0   1/4   1/2   1 mile

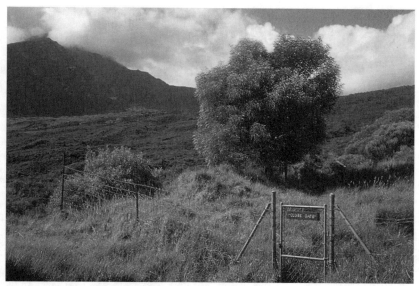

Park boundary, Kaupo Trail

The better approach is from Ulupalakua, though it's a long and, beyond Keokea, a very slow drive. Allow at least 2 hours each way for this drive and have a full tank of gas before you start out. When the Kaupo Store is open (see above), you can get food and drink there; otherwise, take them with you. I'd prefer to have recommended that you make this a side trip from someplace closer than Wailuku. But there are few accommodations—try bed-and-breakfast services to find a place in Kula—and no legal campgrounds on the route between Kahului and the campground at Kipahulu. So it's drive, drive, drive; hike, hike, hike; drive, drive, drive. It's worth it!

From Wailuku, drive east on Highway 32 to Highway 36. Take Highway 36 southeast and then northeast to Highway 37. Turn onto Highway 37 southeast through Pukalani; stay on Highway 37 where Highway 337 departs toward Haleakala's summit (both times). Follow it southeast, then south and southwest, through the rolling green slopes of "upcountry" Maui (Kula, Waiakoa, Keokea, and Ulupalakua Ranch). Keokea is your last chance for gas!

Beyond Ulupalakua Ranch, the road is renumbered as Highway 31 and bears east. It becomes narrower; you may wish to pull over to let others pass from time to time. Compared to its previous condition, the road has been improved considerably for some miles, though you may

Kaupo church

still encounter very rough, narrow stretches. Speeds are 20-25 mph tops. You descend gradually to the coast, and the pavement ends a little before Kaupo. You pass the Kaupo Store (see above) between mile markers 34 and 35. *Please do not park for your hike at the Kaupo Store!* By all means resupply there, but you can then drive another 1.6 miles and 720 feet up to the real trailhead. In 0.1 mile beyond the Kaupo Store you pass a private driveway and reach an unpaved road just before a sign giving the mileage to the park's Kipahulu District. Turn left onto the partly paved road, which is narrow and rough but passable. Follow the road uphill for 1.5 miles, to its end where there is a fork: right to a house, sharply left to a grassy area where there's informal parking for a few cars and beyond that a stone wall. Bear left and park as best you can—it's pretty uneven ground—51.5 long and beautiful miles from Wailuku. Don't block the right fork or the house. There's a trailhead sign for Haleakala National Park near a gate in the stone wall.

Permit/permission required: None.

Description: Following the road, you walk from the parking lot toward the trailhead sign and through the gate in the stone wall. A sign a few yards past the gate advises you that you may go no farther on the road but must pick up the trail to your right (northwest). If the trail is overgrown, it's slow going as you pass avocado, castor, silk oak, and a smelly trash heap. Because the path is faint, numerous little TRAIL signs help point it out—but be aware that the signs are oriented to help people hiking *down* this trail from Haleakala "crater," not those hiking *up* it! This part of the trail can be tough, but the rewards—the views ahead—are worth the trouble, I think. Many use trails and cow paths crisscross the area, petering out in the thickets and adding to the confusion. If you find yourself bushwhacking for more than 10 feet, you've lost the true trail; backtrack before you get lost in the dense growth off-trail. Your goal is to reach the old 4WD road shown on the map as "Kaupo Trail."

Cross an intermittent stream (may be dry) and ascend a slope, bashing your way through the undergrowth. Climb over a stile and begin working your way uphill following signs. After veering into some *kukui* trees, walk up a north trending gully that's also a cow path. Especially if the signs are gone, cross a little ridge before descending toward a cattle-watering area—probably with cattle. As the trail hooks northwest, two shallow gullies appear, one trending northwest and the other more northerly. Follow signs or take the path/cow-track up the more northerly gully, eventually curving over another ridge, crossing another gully and then climbing steeply along the gully's edge to cross a second stile. Veer right and meet a 4WD road at ½ mile.

Down the road to the right, a sign on a gate advises do not enter. You turn left toward a national-park sign half-hidden in the vegetation (the distance it gives to the park's boundary is too short). In spite of the road's steepness and rockiness, it's a big relief from the bushwhacking you've been doing and offers great views and cool breezes after it breaks free of the trees that here overhang it. You may see tracks branching off the road. Don't take them; stick to the road. Be alert for any vehicles—vehicles are infrequent, but traction on this steep, rocky road can be poor.

At 1⅝ miles, and 1680 feet, the road forks and a trail sign indicates the official route. You may stay on the road or take the official, trail route, which is sometimes too overgrown to follow:

Official trail route: The book's map does not show this trail; it shows the road. Following the TRAIL sign, leave the road to angle right and upward to cross small, grassy meadows and brush past lantana bushes. You pass a water tank and hop over a water pipe a couple of times as you climb moderately on a grassy track through guava and Christmas berry. Presently the trail curves left through a fence, passe another water tank, and then ascends along a water pipe to a switchback turn. It may be apparent by this time that you're on an old, disused road—or it may have become so overgrown that it's just a footpath now. At the top of the switchback leg, you meet the real 4WD road and bear right on it at 2280 feet.

On-the-road route: Take the left fork uphill past a water tank. You'll want to stop often to catch your breath on this steep trail and to enjoy the marvelous views in every direction. The Official Trail rejoins the road at 2280 feet.

Continuing up the road, you approach the 2⅝-mile point, the road forks twice. Take the left fork both times. At a faint, false fork shortly thereafter, bear right on the "main" road. Go left at the next two forks. At the 2⅝-mile point, the maw of cloud-filled Kaupo Gap opens far uphill, and the peak named Haleakala rises on the Gap's west side. As you continue you glimpse a patch of bare, red soil ahead. The road turns to parallel the patch of soil, carrying you into the shade of some *koa* trees, remnants of the forest that once clothed the upper slopes of Haleakala. You pass the ruins of a water tank on your left.

At 3¼ miles, you reach the fence that now surrounds much of Haleakala National Park. There are hitching rails inside and outside the gate. A little flat area shaded by *koa* trees offers you a resting spot just outside the gate. Just inside the fence, a handsome grove of *koa* trees beckons you. If you go through the gate, please be sure you close it, even if you have to stamp down the grass to do it! Don't trip on the gate's threshold bar.

This trip ends here at the boundary of Haleakala National Park at 3840 feet. Retrace your steps from here to your car. (Hikers who want to continue to Paliku Cabin should have a *Nahiku* 7½' topo and should reverse the steps of Trip H7.)

Now the road begins a definite descent to the coast, snaking in and out of the narrow throat of deep Manawainui Gulch. As you approach Kaupo, the green of trees softens the harsh landscape. Stretches of paved road alternate with unpaved road until the pavement ends for good. At last you pass lonely, picturesque St. Joseph's Church and, a little farther on, reach the Kaupo Store. Kaupo is beautifully green, swept clean by strong breezes, and tranquil in a way you're not likely to find elsewhere on Maui. Unlike Hana, Kaupo remains truly remote, difficult to reach, and little-visited.

Enjoy your hike and then leave quietly, thankful that there's still a place like Kaupo.

The Road to Kaupo

Cool, green "upcountry" is a treat for the eye and a welcome change from the heat of Lahaina and Kihei. The eucalyptus-shaded fields and rolling green hills with their views down to the sea will seem very familiar if you've spent any time along the coast of central California.

A drastic change occurs after you pass Ulupalakua: the green pastures of "upcountry" soon disappear, and you find yourself driving through a landscape scorched, barren, and colorless in the fierce light. You drive past the sunstruck Lualailua Hills and between the grazing lands of huge ranches. Cattle, stupefied by the heat and dazed by the glare, sag against splintering chutes and huddle in the pitiful shade of leafless *wiliwili* trees. Along the road, apple-of-Sodom's yellow fruit dangles fat and deadly from its withered parent.

These parched slopes once supported sizeable human populations. Not far from the Lualailua Hills and upslope of the highway lie the ruins of Kahikinui, where a thousand or more people once lived. *Maui: How It Came To Be* notes that there are more than 140 house-sites in ruins between Ulupalakua and Kaupo. This area was heavily populated when Cook arrived in Hawaii in 1778. But soon after, the goats, cattle, and pigs descended from those brought by Europeans began stripping the land of its vegetation. It was naturally arid to start with; now, with insufficient vegetation to trap and retain what little moisture fell, it became a desert. The damage continues today; a way to successfully control the animals still hasn't been worked out (except for Haleakala's fences).

Trip E15

Waihou Spring Trail

Distance	Elevation gain	Hiking time	Topos
2 miles	480' (Loss/gain)	1 hour	Kilohana 7½'

Difficulty: Moderate, hiking boots strongly recommended.

Highlights: A pleasant stroll takes you through dry forest and down into a fern-shaded gully, where the spring is probably dry but it's mighty pretty, anyway. The drive to and from the trailhead is a treat all by itself—Maui's Upcountry is so beautiful!

Driving instructions: From Wailuku, drive east on Highway 32 to its junction with Highway 36 (the Hana Highway). Turn southeast (right) on Highway 36 and follow it to the junction with Highway 37 (the Haleakala Highway). Turn right onto Highway 37 and follow it to its junction with highway 365 between I Pukalani and Makawao. Turn left into lovely Makawao on what's now Makawao Road. Drive through Makawao's main business district to a junction with Olinda Road. Turn right on Olinda Road and follow this beautiful, narrow, winding road 4.7 miles uphill, past the Maui Bird Conservation Center on the left—not open to the public. Don't hesitate to use the car's lower "gears." Continue 0.3 mile more, past a wide area of red dirt on your right and almost to a modest sign, TREE GROWN RESEARCH AREA, by a dirt road that heads off at right angles to Olinda Road. You'll see a gate and trail signs just a few steps down the dirt road. There's plenty of parking if cars pull in at right angles to the fence, 19.3 miles from Wailuku.

Permit/permission required: None.

Description: The trailhead is at the locked gate across the dirt road. Duck under a hikers' pass-through and wander down the needle-strewn dirt road between rows of tall Monterey pines that stretch away on both sides. There are powerlines on your left and a fence on your right.

The road curves gently south and then west as it rounds a little gully and soon reaches a fork. Go right (ahead, southwest) under mixed pines and swamp mahogany. The trail drops to curve through a tree-filled gully at ¼ mile, then rises as it exits the gully.

Wiliwili

Woody geranium

In a few more steps, you reach the start of the loop part of this trip, which is signed LOOP 0.6 MI, OVERLOOK 0.3 MI, SPRINGS 0.5 MI. Somewhat arbitrarily, go right (northwest) between *aala* trees, pines, and swamp mahogany, toward the "spring." You'll shortly reach another junction where you'll go right again (northwest again) on the out-and-back leg to the spring.

Now you curve west, descending moderately to gradually, to the half-mile mark. Here you drop steeply down a ridge to a shady flat called "Overlook," where there's a bench but far too many trees for good views. Still, it's a very nice rest spot, and the soft Upcountry air of Maui is fragrant with the scents of pine and eucalyptus. There's a large, forested gully northwest of this spot, and it's into this gully that the trail next takes you.

The trail hooks sharply to the right just beyond the bench and begins a steep descent on switchbacks too short and numerous to show on the map in this book. At nearly a mile, you find yourself at the trail's official end, deep in a fern- and tree-shaded grotto surrounded by dark, mossy cliffs. A few steps beyond the trail's end there may be a spring—or not. Numerous tunnels cut into the grotto's cliffs were for diverting water, which may explain why the spring is often dry.

Now retrace your steps to the Overlook and then to the previous junction where you started the out-and-back leg to the spring. Turn right (southwest) here to continue the loop on a broad, forested trail thickly covered with leaves and needles. Soon you curve along the other side of the ridge, and then you wind through some redwoods. A little gully to your right flattens out and disappears a little before you make a very shallow right-left zigzag and resume descending gently.

Nearing 1⅔ miles, you curve generally west along a ridgeline above another small gully and soon close the loop. Turn right here and retrace your steps to the trailhead at just over 2 miles.

Trip E16

Ranger's Cabin
Side Trip from Polipoli

Distance	Elevation gain	Hiking time	Topos
3½ miles	880′	1¾ hours	Lualailua Hills 7½′, Makena 7½′ (Optional)

Difficulty: *Moderate, tennis shoes recommended*

Alert: *Be aware that you may have to share Polipoli's trails with mountain bikers, a situation I regard as hazardous to and unpleasant for hikers.*

Highlights: *I have a surprise for you at the end of this trip, and I don't want to spoil it here!*

Driving instructions: Allow 1½–2 hours for the drive. Polipoli State Park is so remote, partly because of the poor road to it, that it's almost mandatory that you stay overnight there. From Wailuku, drive east on Highway 32 to Highway 36. Take Highway 36 southeast and northeast to Highway 37. Take Highway 37 southeast through Puka-lani and past the first (northern) junction with Highway 377 to the second (southern) junction with Highway 377, 19 miles. Turn onto Highway 377 (a very hard left) and drive ⅓ mile more to a junction with ill-marked Waipoli Road on your right. It's the first road on your right that has a STOP sign. Turn right onto Waipoli Road.

Getting to Polipoli will take you another hour from here. Drive uphill on this road, ignoring side roads and driveways on your right. The road becomes quite steep, narrow (one lane; be alert for oncoming vehicles), and winding (one hairpin turn after another). Cattle graze alongside it; watch out for cattle straying onto the road. After 6 miles from the start of Waipoli Road, the pavement ends and the road, though less winding and steep now, is quite rough (protruding rocks and roots; sometimes deep dust, sometimes hard, slippery clay). Your rental-car company does not want you to drive this section, but, with care, it is sometimes just passable to ordinary passenger vehicles. The road forks 9½ miles from its start; bear right on the fork that dips downhill, negotiating a particularly rocky hairpin on the remaining ½ mile to Polipoli State Park's picnic and camping area. Park here, 29⅓ miles from Wailuku.

If the road is impassable, park on the shoulder near the end of the pavement and treat the rest of the drive as a hike—it can be a very pleasant one in spite of the occasional car or bike.

Permit/permission required: None.

Description: From the campground, backtrack a few steps through the parking lot and up the road to the side road that turns off north-northwest toward the cabin (left if your back is to the campground). You descend this road and soon reach the cabin and, following the signed REDWOOD TRAIL, curve around it to an opening in a fence.

The damp trail descends gently under conifers—look out for exposed roots on the path and for overhanging dead, cone-studded branches! This profusion of dead branches still on the tree, as well as many of the fallen trees, gives the path that oppressive feeling of decay so characteristic of this forest. Most of the trees at the start are cypresses, but there are more and more redwoods as you descend. You twine down into the forest, eventually bearing west. A little beyond ⅔ mile, a spur trail leads uphill on your left to one Polipoli's shelter huts (see below). Just beyond ¾ mile, you reach a junction with the Tie Trail. Here, you and the Redwood Trail turn right and go north-northeast toward the old ranger's cabin. Be alert for false trails as the Redwood Trail bears north.

Eventually, the Redwood Trail curves west. A few more steps brings you to the hydrangea-filled yard of the decaying "ranger's cabin". The hydrangea display can be quite spectacular here—almost as if you had stepped into a gigantic bouquet.

Sooner or later, you have to tear yourself away from the hydrangeas and retrace your steps.

Polipoli State Park

This park is a wonderful resource for the people of Maui but not for visitors from the mainland, especially as you must share the trails with mountain bikers.

There are three memorable hikes from Polipoli in this book: this one, E16, the Ranger's Cabin (which incorporates the forgettable Redwood Trail); E17, Kahua Road; and E18, Skyline Trail, which is also accessible from the summit of Haleakala. The other trails, including the hike known as the Polipoli Loop, are summarized in Appendix B of this book and are not worth your trouble, as explained below.

If you do hike in the heart of Polipoli, make sure you get back to your camp or car before sunset. The Hawaiian twilight is as dark as night there, a bright moon can't penetrate the forest except at rare clearings, and a flashlight is no substitute for daylight in that dense growth and on those faint trails. (You should carry one, anyway.)

Staying at Polipoli

Polipoli State Park is very remote, very wet, and very cold compared to the rest of Maui. (It lies in a local low spot within Haleakala's inversion-layer cloud bank.) Your choices when you stay overnight there are its tiny tent-campground or its one cabin (reserved through the Division of State Parks; book well in advance). Drinking water is available only at the tent-campground and the cabin. The shelters

Trip E16

5095
Ranger's Cabin
CCC
Bunkhouse

BOUNDARY TRAIL*

*Trails *not* recommended:
uninteresting, or difficult-to-impossible to follow, or (in most cases) both.

N

PLUM TRAIL*

REDWOOD

TIE TRAIL*

Shelter

TRAIL

POLIPOLI

STATE

PARK

Puu Keokea

Polipoli Road

SKYLINE TRAIL

Kahua Road

Start/end
Trip E16-18

POLIPOLI TRAIL*

"Ballpark
Junction"

PLUM TRAIL*

RIDGE

TRAIL*

Polipoli 6472

HALEAKALA

0   1/4   1/2   1 mile

along the trails do not merit your consideration. They are either windowless wooden huts with no light, no water, four dirty wooden bunks, and dirt—I mean loose dirt!—floors, or they are claustrophobic caves. Your tent is a palace compared to those shelters.

Your tent must be waterproof, as it rains frequently at Polipoli and is always damp there. You'll need a warm sleeping bag, rain gear, and plenty of warm clothing. The nearest lodgings are in Kula on Highway 377, but even from there, it's an hour-long grind each way to/from Polipoli.

Kahua Road
Side Trip from Polipoli

Distance	Elevation gain	Hiking time	Topos
9 miles	1210'	4½ hours	Lualailua Hills 7½'

Difficulty: *Strenuous, hiking boots strongly recommended*

Highlights: *Easy going through native scrublands on an old 4WD road with views upslope to Haleakala's summit region and downslope to the ocean (weather permitting). This is by far the most enjoyable of the trails that are accessible only from Polipoli State Park (more below). Kahua Road is a fine choice for mountain bicycles, too.*

Driving instructions: Not applicable if you're already camped at Polipoli State Park. Otherwise, follow the driving instructions of Trip E16.

Permit/permission required: None.

Description: You could start this trip on Polipoli's poor trail system, but I found it much more enjoyable to start on the road. I think you will, too. Get an early start so you can enjoy the views before the fog moves in (it will probably be in a layer just below the road).

Walk back ½ mile on the road you drove in on, to the fork where you turned right to get down to Polipoli. Take the other fork here (a sharp right) and continue uphill. The elbow of a hairpin turn at 1 mile from the start offers wonderful views over the ocean to Molokini and Kahoolawe, even a glimpse of the Big Island of Hawaii, if cloud-cover permits. One of Polipoli's trails, the Haleakala Ridge Trail, meets the road at this elbow.

Volcanic material lies exposed in the road cut, in some places as stacks of wafer-thin orange, black, and tan layers. Near 2 miles, you reach a fork in the road at what's called Ballpark Junction. (The Civilian Conservation Corps men who planted the present forest in the 1930s used to play softball on this flat, open spot.) Kahua Road is the righthand fork, which you take (the lefthand fork is Skyline Trail to Science City atop Haleakala—see Trip E17).

On Kahua Road now, you ignore roads bearing left and right off Kahua Road just beyond Ballpark Junction, and also ignore any tracks leading away from the road, which rises very gently as it heads generally east. The non-native forest soon disappears, and native plants begin to dominate, particularly red- and white-berried *pukiawe*, red-fruited *aalii*, and red-berried *ohelo*. Be sure to look up at that wonderful line of cinder cones along Haleakala's southwest rift zone from time to time—quite a sight! The road passes through flows of rough *aa* lava as clouds move constantly across the slopes, now hiding, now revealing, but always leaving a strip of blue sky somewhere. Cool breezes make this exposed road quite pleasant. Here and there, masses of concrete lie broken where there's been an unsuccessful attempt to smooth the road's rough surface. You'll also notice the occasional rain-collecting station's roofs and tanks.

A little less than ½ mile from Ballpark Junction, you reach a fence with two vehicle gates, one pedestrian gate, and a sign that says HAWAI-

Trip E17 continues next page

Kanahou
VABM △
8653

N

1 mile

1/4   1/2

0

SKYLINE TRAIL

KAHUA ROAD

"Ballpark Junction"

Polipoli Road

Puu Keokea

POLIPOLI STATE PARK

TRAIL

REDWOOD

Shelter

TIE TRAIL *

PLUM TRAIL *

Trip E16

BOUNDARY TRAIL *

*Trails *not* recommended: uninteresting, or difficult-to-impossible to follow, or (in most cases) both.

5095
Ranger's Cabin ★
CCC Bunkhouse

Start/end Trips E16-E18 [T]

POLIPOLI TRAIL *

RIDGE TRAIL *

△ Polipoli 6472

PLUM TRAIL *

HALEAKALA

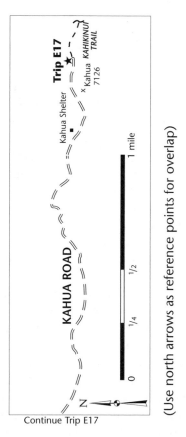

Continue Trip E17

(Use north arrows as reference points for overlap)

IAN HOME LANDS KAHIKINUI. There's a hunter's check station on the seaward side of the road just beyond the fence. Go through the pedestrian gate, being careful to close and latch it behind you. Continue your hike; be sure to stay on the road.

A little past 3 miles, the road begins an almost imperceptible descent, cutting through low ridges of brown *aa* that extend like misshapen fingers toward the distant sea. Scrub and bracken fern happily colonize them. It's not long before you can see a bit of the white towers and domes of Science City, the research complex atop Haleakala, uphill and to the left (northeast), if weather permits. The slopes below Science City are streaked with colors: brick reds, browns, deep maroons, tans, touches of pink and orange, and the green of vegetation.

You've been seeing lots of *aa* lava, but just past 4 miles, there's a smooth *pahoehoe* lava flow. A little farther on you'll find Kahua shelter (on the left side of the road; water available outside) and a pit toilet and Kahua cone (on the right). The deteriorating road passes behind Kahua cone and ends at a trashed-out grassy area 4½ miles from Polipoli. A footpath, the Kahikinui Trail, takes off east-southeast from here through the lava fields; its start is marked only by a couple of metal poles (more about the Kahikinui Trail below).

From here you retrace your path back to Polipoli.

Kahikinui Trail

This is an interesting and very rugged use trail. It's so remote that if you wish to explore it, you should backpack out to the end of Kahua Road and camp near Kahua shelter, sharing its pit toilet and drinking water supply with anyone staying in the shelter. That would give you time to really enjoy the Kahikinui Trail. Check with the Division of Forestry and Wildlife for permission to camp out there (or, at least, assurance that it's okay to do so).

I explored the Kahikinui Trail for about 1½ miles, probably as far as Manawainui Gulch, but not to its end (at least another ½ mile), for lack of time. There were not enough landmarks I could recognize in order to better determine my location at my turnaround point.

The use trail leads across the pleated southern slopes of Haleakala some 5000 to 6000 feet above the scorched countryside through which Highway 31 passes as it goes from Ulupalakua to Kaupo. This is a hunting area, and trash from hunting parties litters the track. The trail occasionally becomes quite hard to follow, so you need to orient yourself with the large cairns (piles of rocks) built on the larger ridges. At times you need to employ your boulder-scrambling skills. You climb over one lava ridge and descend into the gully beyond it, climb out of the gully onto the next lava ridge and descend into the next gully. That might seem monotonous, but something interesting unfolds: the farther you go, the larger and deeper the gullies are, and they begin to hold pools and even streams of water. The floors of the deeper gullies are very smooth in contrast to the rough *aa* of the ridges, and there are interesting formations in some of them. As the gullies become more moist, they provide a niche where soil has accumulated and red-flowered *ohia* trees have taken root. Successive niches seem to support a wider variety of plants. I don't know what you'll find at its end or how you'll know you've reached the end. A current rumor says that the Kahikinui Trail may be extended even farther, perhaps by volunteers, but for now the Kahikinui Trail is near the bottom of the priority list.

See the supplemental information at the end of Trip E14 for a brief look at the ecology and history of these slopes.

Trip E18

Skyline Trail

Side Trip from Polipoli

Distance	Elevation gain	Hiking time	Topos
13 miles	3730'	6½ hours	Lualailua Hills, Kilohana 7½'

Difficulty: *Strenuous, hiking boots strongly recommended*

Highlights: *This thrilling walk up Haleakala's southwest rift zone to Science City, the research complex atop Haleakala, offers sweeping views along Haleakala's slopes and down over the isthmus to West Maui (weather permitting). The contrast between the overgrown Polipoli region at the start and the lava moonscape at the top is startling. Nearing the top, the road wanders among cinder cones and vents—at least one big vent opens almost at your feet. Most of the Skyline Trail is now closed to motorized traffic, so it makes an outstanding hiking and*

173

mountain-bicycling trail. This would be the way to bike down Hale-akala—no dodging the stream of passenger vehicles! Of course, you can also hike or bike the Skyline Trail down from Science City and then back up (see the end of Trip H18). If starting from Science City, park at Red Hill (Trip H18) and walk back down the road, facing traffic, to the Skyline Trail's upper end.

Driving instructions: Not applicable if you're already camped at Polipoli State Park. Otherwise, follow the driving instructions of Trip E16.

Permit/permission required: None.

Description: Follow Trip E17 to Ballpark Junction. Take the left fork and climb moderately past orange-berried *pilo*, yellow-flowered *mamane*, *pukiawe*, *ohelo*, bracken fern, and dubautia. Note the dubautia, with its composite brush of yellow florets. It's a relative of the silversword (hard to believe, but it's true; more on this following Trip H11). One-quarter mile beyond Ballpark Junction, you pass the upper end of the new Mamane Trail (not on map), a hiking-and-mountain-biking trail that's still under construction and that I haven't hiked and don't plan to (I don't like sharing single-track trails with mountain bikes). The Mamane Trail veers off to the left, north-northwest, but you go right (ahead), staying on the road that's the Skyline Trail.

The Skyline Trail stays on the northwest side of the rift zone most of the time. On the ridge to your right, the line of red-brown cinder cones marches along the rift itself. Early in the morning, you have breathtaking views downslope across "upcountry," where plantings of conifers look like so many toy Christmas trees. You'll notice the occasional rain-catching station, too (roof, tanks). Many roadside cuts display colorful layers of volcanic soil. It's possible you'll see wild pigs here, along with ring-necked pheasants. Non-native evening primrose (large, loose, yellow flowers) and thistle put in an appearance, too.

You can't help but notice as you rise higher and higher that the vegetation becomes smaller and sparser. At 3¾ miles you pass around a gate that bars further travel to motorized vehicles, and soon the larger shrubs disappear. Nearing 5 miles, only *pukiawe* remains, in low, compact mounds. Up here, the ground is covered with red, gray, orange, and pink volcanic cinders. On them lie raw chunks of red and black-red rock—"lava bombs," masses of lava ejected from the adjacent vents. Here and there between the heaps of lava grow strange little

Line of craters, Skyline Trail

alpine meadows of tough straw-colored grasses, low dubautias, and diminutive bracken ferns. The jagged mouths of vents gape north and east of you. As tempting as it may be, exploring lava fields off-road or off-trail can be hazardous without a knowledgeable guide. You could unknowingly step right through the fragile roof of an unseen lava tube. Mountain-bicyclists should carefully control their speed on this section, where the roadbed consists of very loose material.

As you approach Science City, avoid turnoffs to its facilities and continue generally northeast toward Red Hill, which is Haleakala's summit. You leave Kahikinui State Forest Reserve at 6 miles and pass around the upper road-closure gate just before 6½ miles. Another few steps bring you to the Skyline Trail marker for the upper (Science City) end. Depending on your fancy and the weather, you may want to find a spot in the cinders near here to rest, enjoy the available views, and have lunch. Or you may want to continue carefully up the road to the observation shelter at Red Hill, visible straight ahead now (additional mileage and elevation gain not included in the figures for this trip).

When you're ready, retrace your steps back to Polipoli.

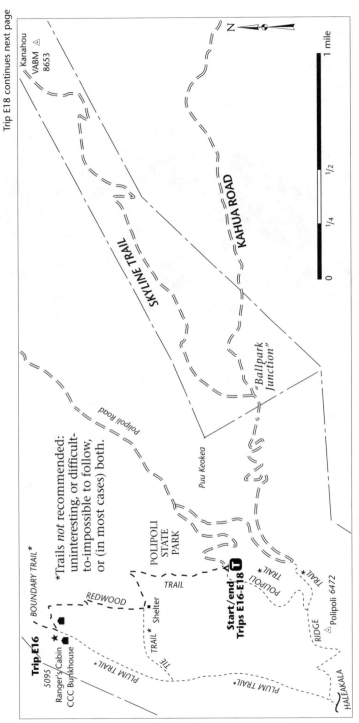

Trip E18 continues next page

Kanahou
VABM △
8653

N

SKYLINE TRAIL

KAHUA ROAD

"Ballpark
Junction"

Puu Keokea

Polipoli Road

POLIPOLI
STATE
PARK

△
TRAIL

Shelter

Start/end
Trips E16-E18 T

POLIPOLI
TRAIL*

RIDGE
TRAIL*

△ Polipoli 6472

*Trails *not* recommended:
uninteresting, or difficult-
to-impossible to follow,
or (in most cases) both.

Trip E16
5095
Ranger's Cabin
CCC Bunkhouse
★

REDWOOD
, BOUNDARY TRAIL*

TIE
TRAIL*

PLUM TRAIL*

PLUM TRAIL*

HALEAKALA

0   ¼   ½   1 mile

HALEA-
KALA N.P.

Red
Hill
10023 x

Satellite
Tracking
Station

Radio
Facility

**Trip
E18**

(est.)

SKYLINE TRAIL

Radio Facility

Radio Tower

KAHIKINUI
FOREST
RESERVE

1 mile

Kalepeamoa

Trip E18

9108

1/2

1/4

0

SKYLINE TRAIL

N

Kanahou
VABM △
8653

Continue Trip E18

177

Why are Puu Kukui and Haleakala so different?

As you walked up from Polipoli, you probably had good views of West Maui until the daily cloud layer formed. Puu Kukui, the volcano that created West Maui, is one of the wettest spots on earth, as its deeply eroded contours brilliant with dense rainforest growth attest. For rainfall, Puu Kukui (5788 feet) rivals Kauai's Mt. Waialeale (5148 feet), which is considered by some to be the rainiest spot on earth. Puu Kukui and Mt. Waialeale have features in common that make them so rainy. Continuing on the Skyline Trail, you then walked up through scrublands and into the alpine desert near the top of Haleakala, where only a few low plants are tough enough to survive. How different Puu Kukui and Haleakala are! But why? In *Hawaii: A Natural History*, Sherwin Carlquist gives an explanation that I've tried to summarize here.

First, an oversimplified look at the air over Hawaii: The Hawaiian Islands tend to have daytime inversion layers 50% to 70% of the time. In these inversion layers, the air gets warmer as it rises (the land heats it). The top of the inversion layer is at 5000 to 7000 feet. Above, there's cooler air. Second, the incoming winds, both trade and kona, pick up a great deal of moisture on their long sweep across the open ocean to Hawaii. The winds rise, warming instead of cooling as they rise, until they encounter the cooler air at the top of the inversion layer. There their moisture condenses as rain.

If the mountain is rounded and its summit is at about the height of the inversion layer, the moisture-laden air rises gradually. The moisture condenses as it rises up and over the summit. There's time for rain to fall on the windward and leeward sides as well as on the summit.

That doesn't happen with Puu Kukui and Waialeale, even though both summits are at about the height of the inversion layer. Both mountains have rainfall concentrated near the summit and have dry leeward sides because both mountains are *not* rounded. They're gashed on all sides by deep, narrow valleys that have very steep headwalls. The moisture-laden winds rush into those valleys and fly up the steep headwalls so rapidly that the air mass is almost at the summit when the moisture condenses very abruptly. Most of the rain falls on the summit ridge and just beyond the summit, effectively concentrating the rainfall in a relatively small region. Immense swamps lie just beyond these summits.

If the mountain is significantly higher than the inversion layer, the rain falls largely on the windward side, leaving both the summit and the leeward side dry. This is the case with 10,023-foot Haleakala. You can almost see the top of the inversion layer around Haleakala. A cloud layer typically forms in the morning and surrounds the mountain at about 5000 to 7000 feet on most sides. Polipoli State Park at 6200 feet on the western slopes lies within this cloud belt, and it is usually very foggy, often rainy, by mid-morning. Above the inversion layer lie the drier scrublands and the alpine deserts you walk through on the Skyline Trail.

The Skyline Trail, with its views of Puu Kukui, offers a fine lesson about Maui's "weather makers" and their effects—a lesson you can take with you to help you better understand the other Hawaiian islands, too.

Lava debris, Skyline Drive

Trip E19

King's Highway to Kanaio

Distance	Elevation gain	Hiking time	Topos
4 miles	40'	2 hours	Makena 7½'

Difficulty: Moderate, hiking boots mandatory

Highlights: An unforgettable panorama: the dazzling turquoise-blue of the water along this coast as seen across the tormented aa landscape left by Haleakala's most-recent eruptions.

Driving instructions: From Wailuku, drive south on Highway 30 to its junction with Highway 31 and follow it past Maalaea Beach and Kealia Pond. As you pass the northernmost condominiums in Kihei, the highway swings slightly inland at a junction with South Kihei Road, 8½ miles from Wailuku. Turn right onto South Kihei Road and follow it south through Kihei. As you approach Wailea, you turn inland (left) a short way on Okolani Drive, then right on Wailea Alanui. You pass several large resorts and golf courses as the road becomes Makena Alanui. As you near the end of the Makena Golf Course, the road becomes very narrow, and thickets of *kiawe* stretch away on either side of the road. You pass a couple of dirt roads leading seaward to Puu Olai (Trip E20). The road is alternately paved and unpaved now—more often paved—and bobs up and down. You may not be able to see traffic on the other side of these "mounds," so exercise caution.

The road presently dips down to skirt Ahihi Bay and then crosses the base of Cape Kinau to a small parking area just past a memorial to La Pérouse—a truncated pyramid inland—and below Puu o Kanaloa at the northwest end of La Pérouse Bay. From here the "road" is impassable to all but the stoutest 4WD vehicles and to the Ankle Express, so park here to begin your hike, 23¼ miles from Wailuku.

Permit/permission required: None.

Description: The heat from sun, reradiated by the dark lava rocks along this route, can be intense, and there is no fresh water. From the parking area, pick up the extremely rough 4WD road that bears southeast over *aa* and under *kiawe* to skirt La Pérouse Bay—don't take the spur road that goes south to the sea. There are wonderful views over the blue-green bay toward Kahoolawe and up the slopes of Haleakala, down which streams of rough, dark lava have poured. You may notice some beaten paths through the *aa*, but these are not your trail. At a junction in less than ⅕ mile where another jeep road peels off seaward, you continue ahead. The road soon becomes sandy and begins winding in and out of tiny, rocky coves under a natural archway of *kiawe*. Inland, growing *kiawe* and castor bean push apart the lichen-speckled boulders of old stone walls.

The road becomes alternately rocky and sandy, and *hau* and *noni* appear as you pass the ½-mile point and reach a striking cove backed by *kiawe* and with a little beach. At a junction (not on the map) on the far side of the cove, take the right (south-southeast) fork through an open area of reddish *aa* and past a square stone enclosure seaward of your route. Inland, you notice a stone wall and wire fence. Look for a pedestrian opening in the fence with a vehicle barrier in the wall and turn left (inland) through the pedestrian opening. Walk about 100 feet to the Hoapili Trail, built in its present form by Governor Hoapili in

The map shows:
- Puu o Kanaloa
- 212
- Keoneoio
- **Start/end Trip E19**
- Cape Kinau
- La Pérouse Bay
- Lae o Papaka
- Cape Hanamanioa
- "THE KING'S HIGHWAY"
- BM 37
- x 48
- Hanamanioa Light
- Kanaio
- **Trip E19**
- Kamanamana
- N
- 0 1/4 1/2 1 mile

1824–1840. (Remember that these lava flows date from about 1790, so they may have destroyed an earlier King's Highway here. See Trip E7 for some background on the King's Highway.) Na Ala Hele, the Hawaiian trail-support organization, has rebuilt Governor Hoapili's "King's Highway" here, and you turn right onto it.

The going is pretty rough now, as the trail consists of *aa* chunks laid to form trailbed but not cemented together, so that they wobble a little under your boots. Soon you reach a second access from the 4WD road and a very official-looking trail sign saying that Kanaio Beach is 2 miles ahead. (No, from here it's 1⅓ miles.) The *aa* wilderness stretches away on all sides, often blocking ocean views. Its origin in the lava flows on the slopes above could hardly be more obvious. *Is this what an ant feels like in a gravel bed?* you may wonder. Still, the tortured rocks are not without their beauty. They are, after all, the raw material from which time and erosion will fashion new, fertile plains. Some of the rocks ring almost bell-like beneath your feet. Stop to examine them.

The broken fragments sometimes reveal delicate, marbled colors and bubble chambers. Grays and browns predominate, but surprising tints appear when you look closely: soft oranges, deep purplish reds, brick reds, ochres, pinks, and the white of lichens called 'Hawaiian snow." Rarely, you may see a smooth lava "bomb."

About half a mile before Kanaio, you spot a tree-shaded cove that the King's Highway bypasses. Just a little farther on, a rough use trail threads its circuitous way down to the cove's gray-sand beach, circumventing a *hau*-filled gully as it passes a stone structure. If Kanaio is crowded, you might decide to come back here. But for now, you stay on the King's Highway. Two miles from your start, you descend very abruptly to a marvelously picturesque, *kiawe*-shaded cove along a coast locally known as Kanaio. There is a trashy campsite here, and a 4WD road comes down to it on the far side. Still, it's a fine place to rest and have lunch. The King's Highway continues a few coves farther on, but this trip ends here. Retrace your steps when you're ready.

Hoapili Trail

Beyond Kanaio

You may want to explore Kanaio a little more before you leave. If you continue along the shore, you'll hear the *WHOOOOOSH!* of a small blowhole if the tide is high enough. (I'll let you have the fun of hunting for it.) Your trail is a 4WD road now; as you approach a ruin on a small point, it turns inland. At a junction with another jeep trail, one that goes inland, you bear right (east), staying along the coast. It becomes rockier and, at 3 miles, dips abruptly down through a stone wall toward the sea.

I cannot recommend the next stretch to Kanaloa. The King's Highway has not been rebuilt here and is extremely rough and hot. You are permitted to backpack this route and to camp along this coast from Kanaio east to Kanaloa, but I can't recommend that, either. There's no fresh water, and the few potential campsites are full of junk.

Cove along Hoapili Trail (King's Highway, Kanaio)

Trip E20

Puu Olai

Distance	Elevation gain	Hiking time	Topos
1½ miles	480′	¾ hour	*Makena 7½′* (Optional)

Difficulty: *Moderate, hiking boots strongly recommended*

Highlights: *Superb views from one of the two summits of this little tree-topped cone, plus an opportunity to visit two beautiful beaches.*

Driving instructions: Get an early start; the parking lot for this popular area is often full by 10 A.M. Start as described in the driving instructions of Trip E19, but don't go all the way to La Pérouse Bay. Instead, as you drive south from Kihei, look for the prominent cone—Puu Olai—that sticks out into the ocean; you can't miss it. A paved

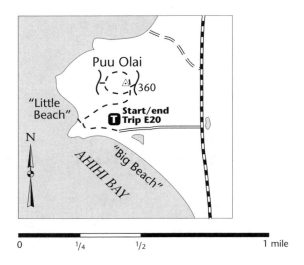

road comes in from the north to join your road, now named Makena Alanui, at a very sharp angle on your right, just as the main road turns away from Makena Golf Course. As you come abreast of Puu Olai, pass the road that heads seaward along Puu Olai's north side. Look for the paved road that heads seaward along Puu Olai's south side to Makena State Park (it may not be marked as such on Makena Alanui). Follow this access road for ⅓ mile to a paved parking area, just under 20½ miles from Wailuku. You can't drive all the way to the beach any more, so park here. The beach is locally called Big Beach; on maps, it's often shown as Oneloa Beach; and now it's Makena State Park. Vandalizing cars is a growth industry here, so be sure to take all your valuables with you.

Permit/permission required: None.

Description: Walk past the vehicle gate at the beach end of the parking lot, then down the remaining road, and bear right past the defunct, elevated restroom, toward the handsome red cliffs framing the north end of the beach. The little point extending from the base of Puu Olai is right ahead of you; walk to its face. Here you'll find a steep use trail hidden in the cliff. You scramble steeply up the low cliff with the help of some natural handholds. When you're atop the cliff, take the time to look back and enjoy the view of Big Beach from here. Side trails lead out onto the point to tidepools, and a wide trail leads northwest (ahead) to Little Beach. You, however, want the very steep use trail on your right that climbs northeast along Puu Olai's southern slopes. Take this trail upward—*upward!*—on loose, cindery soil, through *koa haole* and *kiawe*. Past the ⅓-mile point, the grade eases a little, then steepens again as you pass through weeds, and finally eases for good at an open spot a little over ½ mile from your start.

Here, atop Puu Olai's southeast summit, you have fabulous views southwest to Molokini and Kahoolawe, northwest to West Maui, southeast to Haleakala, and south to the southwest rift zone and Cape Kinau. Now you begin the loop part of this trip by following the use trail north past a slight depression and through scrub, to a fork. Take the left fork, which passes a cement marker (possibly the remains of the benchmark shown on the topo), descends to a saddle, and then climbs to Puu Olai's northwest summit. Though it's slightly higher, this summit's views are obscured by *kiawe* and the southeast summit. Follow the track across this summit as it descends west and then south around Puu Olai's *kiawe*-filled vent. At the low point, you meet a track coming uphill from the west, but you continue south around the crater, ascending to the open spot on the southeast summit.

Big Beach

Big Beach

Retrace your steps down Puu Olai—slippery on this steep grade and loose soil. From here, you can retrace your steps to lovely Big Beach (left as you face the ocean). If you turn to your right, the trail leads to Little Beach in a few dozen yards.

When you're ready, return the way you came, just over 1½ miles total (not including going to Little Beach).

Little Beach

Hawaii's Secret Beaches says that Little Beach is "Hawaii's most well known nudist beach because of the numerous arrests here of nudists." It is beautiful, and, though nudity is officially illegal here because it's in a state park, you'll find people sunning and swimming with and without swimsuits. If nudity offends you, it's best not to go to Little Beach. Nudity isn't legal anywhere in Hawaii, and the law, which once winked at it in a few remote places, is increasingly intolerant of it today.

Trip E21

Polo Beach

Distance	Elevation gain	Hiking time	Topos
⅔ mile	Negligible	20 minutes	*Makena 7½'* (Optional)

Trail map: *There's no trail as such; you just follow the shoreline.*

Difficulty: *Very easy, tennis shoes recommended*

Highlights: *This trip: 1. Gives you an excuse to visit a perfectly lovely beach and to potter around a bit on it, enjoying the views and looking at the plants, maybe sunning and swimming, too. 2. Gives you legitimate grounds for subsequently claiming that you were on a hike the whole time, so it's okay to stop for ice cream on the way back to the condo.*

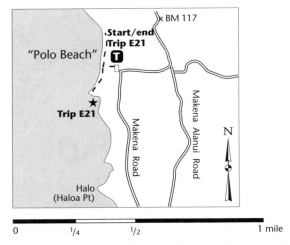

There is no trail as such; you walk along the beach as you please.

Driving instructions: Start as described in the driving instructions of Trip E19. Beyond Kihei, after you've gone briefly uphill and then past some big resorts, keep your eye on the signs pointing to beaches. Turn right where the sign points you seaward to Polo Beach, just over 17 miles from Wailuku and just beyond an elaborate, turreted hotel. It's a block to the end of this short street, where you turn right into the parking lot for Polo Beach. The walkway to the beach is at the far end of the parking lot.

Permit/permission required: None.

Description: Descend the short flight of stairs to the beach and continue walking ahead to the black boulders at the north end of the beach. Chairs, lounges, and umbrellas dot the beach; they belong to the luxury hotel whose grassy lawn extends to the edge of the low bluffs backing this cove. There's a splendid view of West Maui as you go. Several kinds of seaweed grow on just these few boulders; how many of them can you identify? (Sea lettuce was the only one I could identify.)

On the low, sandy bluff backing the beach, you'll find *akulikuli*, beach vitex (*pohinahina*), beach *naupaka* (*naupaka-kahakai*), and *ilima papa*—a nice little collection of naturally occurring plants for an area as developed as this one is. These plants are indigenous to Hawaii's beaches and to many other tropical Pacific coastlines, having arrived in

Hawaii without human assistance. For example, the white fruits of beach *naupaka* are buoyant and tolerant of saltwater, so ocean currents can disperse them from one shoreline to another. According to *Hawaiian Coastal Plants and Scenic Shorelines*, development has taken a heavy toll on Hawaii's beach vitex plants, so it's good to see them flourishing here. *Kiawe* trees and tree heliotrope, both introduced species, grow atop the bluff.

It's only a few steps to the other end of the beach, where you can continue walking by stepping over trailing morning-glory vines and then crossing the black-pebble and white-coral beach of a little cove. A use trail leads from here through *kiawe* to another pebbly cove that offers a fine view of Puu Olai, whose two summits are quite distinct from this vantage point. Out to sea, tiny Molokini lies in front of Kahoolawe, an island sacred in Hawaiian mythology—more about Kahoolawe below.

Return to the beach after taking in these fine views, and retrace your steps to your car when you're ready.

Kahoolawe

Kahoolawe is too small and too arid to support a substantial population, but small family groups inhabited it well into historic times. It became a thriving cattle ranch in the first half of this century. One day after the Japanese attack on Pearl Harbor, the U.S. Navy seized Kahoolawe, dispossesed the ranch owners, and began using the island for target practice. After a long and bitter struggle between the U.S. Navy and Hawaiian groups determined to see the desecration stopped, Congress finally voted in 1990 to return Kahoolawe to Hawaii. Its restoration will be a fascinating project for those lucky enough to participate and an interesting story to follow for the rest of us.

Trip E22

Kamaole County Beach Park 2 and 3

Distance	Elevation gain	Hiking time	Topos
1 mile	Negligible	½ hour	Puu o Kila 7½' (Optional)

Trail map: There's no trail as such; just explore the area.

Difficulty: Very easy, tennis shoes recommended

Highlights: Views, picnic facilities, restrooms, a children's playground, plenty of sandy beach to stroll on and stretch out on, plenty of grass to move onto when that midday Kihei breeze picks up—Kamaole has lots to offer. There are 3 beaches in this park (Kamaole Beach County Parks 1, 2, and 3) separated by private property that you can skirt by walking along the tide-line. Each beach is worth a visit, but I've arbitrarily limited this hike to beaches 2 and 3 because a mile's walk seems just about *right for this area. This trip is better in the morning—you'll avoid the midday wind.*

Driving instructions: Start as described in the driving instructions of Trip E19. In Kihei, keep your eyes peeled after you pass Kalama Beach County Park (seaward side) and Kihei Town Center (a shopping center). First you'll pass Kamaole 1, then some resorts and shopping malls, then Kamaole 2, and finally you'll reach Kamaole 3. Park near Kamaole 3 if possible (this trip starts at the south end of Kamaole 3) or Kamaole 2, 13–13⅓ miles from Wailuku, depending on where you

There is no trail as such; you walk on the beach or on the grass as you please. Just how far you actually walk depends on whether you stick to the beach, detour to the grass, and so on.

park. If you come to a left-hand, uphill jog, you've gone too far; turn around.

Permit/permission required: None.

Description: Start your walk at the south end of Kamaole 3 (left end as you face the ocean). Stroll north (toward West Maui, looming in the distance) on the beach if the wind permits, on the grass if it doesn't. *Kiawe*, palms, and monkeypod trees shade the grass, where you'll also find tables, grills, restrooms, water, and playground equipment. At the north end of Kamaole 3, you'll need to be on the beach, or to detour to it, to circumvent a *kiawe*-covered point the top of which is marked PRIVATE PROPERTY. A use trail along the low bluff below the point allows you to walk around to Kamaole 2 without trespassing. If tide and surf permit, you can walk out on the rocks here, exploring tidepools as you go—best not to do this barefooted!

Soon you're at the sandy south end of Kamaole 2, whose beach is somewhat longer. The pleasant grassy area of Kamaole 2 has no facilities but is brightened by morning glory, beach *naupaka*, autograph tree, and bougainvillea. As you stroll north, the grassy area ends where the buildings begin. The beach stretches farther in front of the buildings, and you may wish to check out Kamaole 1, while others will want to turn around here. Now that you've had a good look at Kamaole, it's time to make your really big decisions: where to stretch out in the sun, and whether to have your picnic lunch now or later. They're tough decisions when you have so many good choices. Maybe you should think it over as you amble back toward Kamaole 3, retracing your steps. In any case, you won't be in any hurry to get back to your car for a while. Enjoy your stay!

Hosmer Grove
Nature Loop

Distance	Elevation gain	Hiking time	Topos
Just under ⅔ mile	120'	Less than 20 minutes	Kilohana 7½' (Optional)

Difficulty: *Very easy, tennis shoes recommended*

Highlights: *A number of native and introduced plants grow together here, and many of them are marked with numbered stakes so that you can identify them with the help of a brochure that should be available at the first numbered station. The brochure also has historical information and poses some intriguing questions about this area. It's a fine little hike even if the brochure isn't available. Birders should bring their binoculars and plan to take advantage of the birding opportunities midway along* *the trail. Best in the early morning, as clouds and rain often move in by midmorning.*

Driving instructions: From Wailuku, drive east on Highway 32 to its junction with Highway 36 (Hana Highway). Take Highway 36 to its junction with Highway 37 (Haleakala Highway). Take Highway 37 through Pukalani—last chance for gas and groceries—to the first junction with Highway 377. Turn left onto Highway 377, which is now the Haleakala Highway, and follow it through the green pasturelands of eucalyptus-shaded "upcountry" to its junction with Highway 378. Turn left onto Highway 378 (*it's* now the Haleakala Highway) and follow it uphill on its zigzagging course toward Haleakala's summit. Just after you cross the park boundary, a sign points left down a side road to Hosmer Grove and its campground, just under 30 miles from Wailuku. Turn left here and follow the side road past a spur road (to a radio facility) to the side road's end in ½ mile at the Hosmer Grove parking lot 30½ miles from Wailuku.

Cattle on the road are hazards drivers must watch out for. Many areas on the slopes along Highways 377 and 378 below the national park are pastures. There's no fence to keep the cattle that graze there from wandering onto the road, so of course they do. You're especially likely to find them on the road in the evening and at night. Be ready to stop for them. They'll amble off the road if you'll give them time.

Permit/permission required: None.

Description: Hosmer Grove, at 6800 feet, is not only high but potentially windy, cold, and wet. Be prepared with warm clothing that insulates when wet, with rain gear, and with shoes that will grip on slippery terrain. And take it easy if you're unaccustomed to hiking at higher altitudes!

Walk toward the trees, past the picnic pavilion, and pick up the path, paved at first, that leads away from the parking lot. As it bears north, you pass an information sign explaining that Hawaii's first territorial forester, Ralph S. Hosmer, planted this grove, now named in his honor, in 1910. The grove consists (like Polipoli) largely of continental species. Hosmer wanted to see if they would flourish here and support a timber industry. Fortunately, they didn't do well enough to compete with imported timber. As the pamphlet you'll pick up at the first station asks, "Do you think Haleakala would be a National Park today if the experiment had succeeded?" You promptly cross a stream—may be dry—on a bridge. Exotic eucalyptuses dominate this first part of the grove. Red-berried *pukiawe*, a typical member of the native shrubland that is the natural cover of these slopes, struggles to survive beneath the huge, exotic trees. A procession of other exotics, beginning with sugi cedars, soon takes over from the eucalyptuses. The native shrubs beneath them are more interesting: *aalii, ohia lehua, mamane,* and more *pukiawe*. The trail twists here and there as it climbs a little, then drops a little.

Soon you reach an open spot, fenced and with interpretive displays, where a bench overlooks a gully and an expanse of native shrub-

Pukiawe

land slopes. Break out your binoculars and your bird-identification guides here and settle down for a look at native and exotic birds. True sandalwoods grow here, too. When you move on, via a short, rocky climb, you're out of the grove proper and in native Hawaiian shrub-land. A few seedlings of the exotic species may sprout here, but the Park Service is committed to pulling them up in order to allow the native plants to flourish. Otherwise, the naturally low native plants here would be shaded to death by the dense, towering exotics—as most of them have been in the grove you just left.

At a signed junction, bear left to stay on the nature trail instead of shortcutting back to the campground. Your ascent continues, first gradually and then moderately up a series of rocky "steps." Before descending, you level out at a rocky spot well above the road and alien grove, with a good view upslope. Now descend past another bench with views of the alien grove and an antenna-topped cone near park headquarters. Now descend a few rocky stairsteps. At an apparent fork, go right on the official trail, which soon levels out and meanders through more native scrub. You resume a gentle descent and reach a fork where you go left, into the grove, avoiding a use trail on your left, and return to close the loop through cedars and eucalyptuses. Cross the stream again and reach the road by the restrooms. The parking lot is just downhill on your right.

The trail soon curves back toward the campground. Near the end, false trails crisscross the main trail, but don't let them distract you. The trail returns to the end of the road you drove in on. Stay to picnic and enjoy the scenery!

Native vs. Non

The Park Service must wage its fight in favor of native species and against exotics not only for plants but also for animals. The upper slopes of Haleakala are now completely fenced so that the Park Service can remove the non-native goats and pigs they find inside the fence with some confidence that another batch of goats and pigs won't immediately invade the park in their place. Inside the fence, native plants are recovering. However, a new threat confronts the park: rabbits have been appearing near the fence.

Waikamoi Preserve

The Nature Conservancy owns and manages Waikamoi Preserve, a native near-rainforest area next to Hosmer Grove. Waikamoi Preserve protects many rare and endangered native birds and plants. Birdwatching is the preserve's main attraction for the visitor. Access is by permit only, and travel is allowed on foot only.

The Nature Conservancy conducts guided hikes from Hosmer Grove into the preserve on a regular basis, currently the second Sunday of each month. Call the preserve manager at (808) 572-7849 to reserve a place on their hike. You'll probably get a recording. I've been assured that the preserve manager does return all calls, but you will need to be within reach of your phone to catch that call.

The National Park Service also conducts "cloud forest" hikes in the preserve; call the Park Service at (808) 572-9306 to get the latest information. Reservations are not required, a donation is suggested. Once in a while, the hike may be canceled because of inclement weather, or for lack of a ranger to conduct the hike, or because too few people showed up (the hike requires a minimum of three people for safety). I recommend that you also call the Park Service the morning of the hike, as early as possible (they're in the office by 7:30 A.M.), to be sure it hasn't been cancelled for either of the first two reasons. Hosmer Grove is probably hours away from where you're staying. There's a problem here: how can you get to Hosmer Grove in time for the hike without starting from your hotel well before 7:30 A.M.? You probably can't. Suggestion: take this book with you and drive toward Hosmer Grove but stop in, say, Pukalani for breakfast and call the Park Service around 7:30 A.M. from there. You'll still have time to get up to Hosmer Grove safely if the "cloud forest" hike is still on. Or, if it's been canceled, you'll have time to choose and take another hike.

You will need to make special arrangements directly with the preserve manager for any other access to Waikamoi Preserve.

Trip H2

Supply Trail to Crater Rim

Distance	Elevation gain	Hiking time	Topos
5⅓ miles	1060′	2⅔ hours	Kilohana 7½′

Difficulty: *Strenuous, hiking boots strongly recommended*

Highlights: *This is the trail mule trains take to resupply the cabins in Haleakala's crater. For the hiker, it offers a close-up look at the native shrublands and breathtaking views downslope to East Maui's northeast coast (weather permitting) and, at its upper end, into the crater itself.*

Driving instructions: Follow the driving instructions of Trip H1. Park at Hosmer Grove or, to be closer to the trailhead, park in the first real parking lot—one with striped spaces, not just a pullout—that you come to on your right as you drive toward Hosmer Grove.

Permit/permission required: None.

Description: Walk back down the road you drove in on, past the spur road to the radio facility, ⅓ mile from Hosmer Grove or 135 yards from nearer parking lot, to the signed trailhead that will be on your left (south-southeast) in a wide, shallow, scrub-filled gully on the Hosmer

Grove side of the pronounced dip in the road. Pick up the trail here and follow it uphill through *mamane, pukiawe, ohelo, pilo,* the silvery, shrubby geranium *hinahina,* and bracken ferns. Nearing ½ mile into this hike, the highway swings to the east and comes very close to the trail but is separated from it by a gully. You shortly cross the lava-floored gully just above what must be a pretty little waterfall when there's water flowing here. Presently, you pass a sign listing the park's rules (on your right). Alien, yellow-flowered evening primrose and dandelion grow here; you'll see them far too often along the trails as well as along the roadside.

The trail makes a rocky ascent between a pair of dark-sided gullies, and then curves northeast to cross the larger gully above another impressive but probably dry waterfall; rainwater may have pooled in the lava's shallow depressions. Hosmer Grove and the radio facility are visible downhill to the north—convenient reference points. As the trail veers uphill and southeast, a highway bridge looms ahead to your right. The highway will be above you, on your right, for a while; do your best to ignore it.

The trail works its way across and up the slope on long, lazy switchbacks on a grade that's rarely more than gradual. Step over a culvert, pass through a stone wall, hop over a pipeline, and enjoy the scenery and abundant native plant life as you amble along.

At 1½ miles, just as it comes within yards of you, the highway switchbacks away from you at last. Cross a service road (not shown on the map or the topo) and pick up the trail directly on the other side of it. You pass a rain shed ahead and some water tanks on your left. The topo shows a rain shed and water tanks on your right (west), but they are now on your left (east). Pause often to take in the magnificent views down Haleakala's northeast slopes all the way to the sea, if the cloud cover permits. You cross intermittent streams, gullies, and a couple of culverts; a fern-lined intermittent streambed at 2 miles is especially pretty. Just beyond 2 miles, there's a meadowy area where the tramping of many feet and hooves has worn multiple tracks deep into the soft soil. Footing is spongy here. A flat-faced, dark peak tinged with green rises ahead of you presently; it bounds the southeast side of the crater's Koolau Gap. You meet the Halemauu Trail at 2½ miles from your start, where a sign points you left to the CRATER. (On your way back, go right down the SUPPLY TRAIL at this junction.) Turn left onto the rocky Halemauu Trail, where *mamane, pukiawe,* bracken fern, and *hinahina* line your route.

Native shrub geranium, *hinahina*

You're descending now, and in a few steps you reach a gate in Haleakala's protective fence. Pass through the gate, being sure to close it behind you. A couple of switchbacks bring down to a sweeping crater view just before the trail makes a third switchback This is your destination for this hike. Find a perch here where you can spend some time to watch the show. On your left, Koolau Gap opens. Clouds often fill it, drifting across the crater floor.

Shifting clouds may reveal a feature for a moment, then hide it again while parting to show another feature. The green, spire-studded cliffs of Leleiwi Pali (*pali* means cliffs) fall steeply away at your feet to a meadow that's more than a thousand feet below. On your left, the Halemauu Trail snakes down, down, down the steep ridge that juts into the crater, and the crater walls rise again across Koolau Gap. Eastward, fantastically colored cinder cones dot the crater floor. It's hard to leave this awesome sight, but you can console yourself with more of those fine views toward the coast as you retrace your steps to Hosmer Grove.

Crater Trips Overview

Visualizing the crater's trail system can be difficult, especially as you're taking your first look at it over the crater rim. It's helpful to think of the network of maintained trails in Haleakala's crater as forming a sloppy letter Y, knocked over onto its left side, with a crooked tail, as shown in the drawing below. One arm of the Y starts at the trailhead for the Halemauu Trail. The other arm of the Y starts at the trailhead for the Sliding Sands Trail. There are a couple of maintained spur trails, and there are three maintained interconnecting trails between the Sliding Sands and the Halemauu trails in the vicinity of Kawilinau. The

To Hosmer Grove

Halemauu Trailhead

Park Headquarters

N

Holua Cabin/ Campground

Silversword Loop

HALEAKALA CRATER AREA

378

*Kawilinau

Paliku Cabin/ Campground

Sliding Sands Trailhead

Ka Lua o Ka Oo

SLIDING SANDS TRAIL

HALEMANU TRAIL

Kapalaoa Cabin

KAUPO GAP TRAIL

0	1	2	3 Kilometers
0		1	2 Miles

*Formerly "Bottomless Pit"

Kaupo Gap Trailhead

205

Haleakala Crater overview

Sliding Sands and the Halemauu trails meet not far from Paliku Cabin/Campground to begin the tail of the Y. Just past Paliku Cabin/-Campground, the tail turns almost 90° south toward Kaupo village.

The trips in this book describe a variety of dayhikes and backpacks in Haleakala's crater covering the current network of maintained trails. There's a trip to each of the cabins/campgrounds and a unique dayhike from each cabin/campground. Call the Park Service about taking one of their guided hikes—a wonderful new program you shouldn't miss. See Appendix A for information on permits and cabin reservations. See the note following Trip H4 for the importance of staying on the maintained trails.

Dayhikes from the crater's rim

Trips H4, H11, H12, H13, and H16 are dayhikes from the crater's rim. The most comprehensive trip is strenuous Trip H16 down the Sliding Sands Trail, through the crater, and out on the Halemauu Trail (requires a car shuttle). It's one of the best hikes in this book and on Maui.

ALERT: A note on the Sliding Sands Trail

Some people consider the Sliding Sands Trail to be too difficult to hike out on because of its "loose" surface. However, hikers in good shape may not agree. The surface has been consolidated to some extent by years of being hiked on; that's certainly the way I found it. My friend Ray Brouillard, who backpacked in and out on the Sliding Sands Trail, reports that he had no problem hiking out. Others report similar experiences. The bottom line: if you're fit, don't let the reputation of the Sliding Sands Trail deter you!

To Holua Cabin/Campground

Trip H4, which you can make as either a dayhike or a backpack, takes you to Holua Cabin/Campground in the northwest corner of the crater. Trip H4 is teamed with Trip H5, which is a dayhike from Holua Cabin/Campground to Kapalaoa Cabin.

To Kapalaoa Cabin

Trip H13, which you can make as either a dayhike or a backpack, takes you to Kapalaoa Cabin. Trip H13 is teamed with Trip H14, which is a dayhike from Kapalaoa Cabin to Holua Cabin/Campground via a somewhat different route from that taken by Trip H5. Or you can reverse part of Trip H5 to make it a dayhike from Kapalaoa Cabin.

Holua Cabin

To Paliku Cabin/Campground.

Trip H6 builds on Trip H4 to take you down the Halemauu Trail from Holua Cabin/Campground to Paliku Cabin/Campground. Trip H6 is teamed with Trip H7, which is a dayhike from Paliku Cabin/-Campground down Kaupo Gap to the park's boundary. Trip H7 thus complements Trip E14, which is a dayhike from Kaupo village up Kaupo Gap to the park's boundary. Trip H15 takes you down the Sliding Sands Trail to Paliku Cabin/Campground with an optional night at Kapalaoa Cabin. It's certainly feasible for the sturdier hiker to backpack all the way to Paliku in one day from either the Halemauu or Sliding Sands trailhead because it's mostly downhill. The trip out—uphill—will be more enjoyable if you stay the night at Holua Cabin/Campground or Kapalaoa Cabin.

The grand crater tour

Trip H17 is "the grand crater tour." You visit each cabin or cabin/-campground on a three-night shuttle trip between the Sliding Sands and the Halemauu trailheads. Sturdy early-birds will be able to make morning dayhikes on some of the other crater trails from Holua Cabin/Campground or from Kapalaoa Cabin (e.g., Trips H5 and H14) and still hike out of the crater in the afternoon.

Kaupo Gap

The backpack from either the Sliding Sands or the Halemauu trailhead all the way across the crater floor and down Kaupo Gap almost to Kaupo village requires an extremely long shuttle. Most visitors will find that shuttle to be very difficult to arrange. You may not camp beyond Paliku Cabin/Campground, and there is no readily available water along the way, not even in Kaupo village. Also, the layout of the crater trails and the short time you're allowed to stay in the crater (3 nights maximum in any 30-day period) means you'll have to choose between the Halemauu *and* Sliding Sands trails. It's just not practical to see the entire crater and hike out down Kaupo Gap. That's why I treated Kaupo Gap in two trips, Trip E14 from Kaupo village up to the park boundary, and Trip H7, a side trip from Paliku Cabin down to the park boundary. You won't need a shuttle, and you'll have more time to enjoy the crater or Kaupo Gap or both.

Trip H3

Halemauu Trail to Crater Rim

Distance	Elevation gain	Hiking time	Topos
1½ miles	260′ (Loss/gain)	¾ hour	Kilohana 7½′

Difficulty: *Easy, tennis shoes recommended*

Highlights: *The spectacular view down into Haleakala's crater is the main attraction on this short hike.*

Driving instructions: Follow the driving instructions of Trip H1 but don't turn off at the side road to Hosmer Grove. Instead, continue up Highway 378 toward the Visitor Center, a little over ¾ mile farther. It's a good idea to stop here for information and to get any books and maps you may need. Back on the road, it's a little less than 3½ more miles to the turnoff to the parking lot for the Halemauu Trail, 34¼ miles from Wailuku.

Several *nene*, the endangered native goose that is the state bird of Hawaii, used to frequent the Halemauu Trail's parking lot. Their antics used to amuse many visitors. Unfortunately, there may be no *nene* at the parking lot any more. Most of the *nene* that used to hang out there got run over by cars, and the Park Service moved the others to safety. The Park Service is now trying to keep the *nene* away from roads and trailheads. Maybe you'll meet some *nene* down in the crater; see below for more about them.

Permit/permission required: None.

Description: The start of the Halemauu Trail is a little deceptive: you'd expect it to lead straight away from the parking lot east toward the crater rim. But in fact, it starts off southeastward, passes an information sign where you may find brochures on the park, and finally angles northeast at a little gully. (Remember this for your return.) Descending gently, you contour briefly around Haleakala's slopes through native shrubland. Yellow-flowered *mamane*, red-berried *ohelo*, and a white-flowered native shrub geranium add interest to the trail. If

Mist creeps through Koolau Gap

the weather permits, you'll have some fine views downslope all the way to the ocean, some 7700 feet below and many miles away.

As you near the ⅔-mile point, you meet the supply trail from Hosmer Grove (Trip H2). From here, you continue ahead on the Halemauu Trail through the gate to the crater-rim viewpoint as described in Trip H2, just under ¾ mile from your start. When you can tear yourself away, retrace your steps.

Nene

This handsome, non-migratory goose is believed to have descended from the migratory Brant and Canada geese that occasionally winter over in the Hawaiian Islands. Unlike their ancestors, the *nene* aren't waterfowl. One of the *nene's* adaptations to this dry habitat is feet that are only partially webbed.

There were once as many as 25,000 *nene* in the islands. But by the early 1950s, it was estimated that there were only 30 wild *nene* left.

Nene

Their habitat had been destroyed by the deforestation that had left so much of Hawaii stripped of her native trees. Introduced animals, particularly mongooses and cats, had destroyed *nene* eggs, chicks, and nesting adults. Concerted efforts in Hawaii and in England have enabled the *nene* to survive in captivity. *Nene* have been reintroduced into the wild here at Haleakala National Park, on the Big Island at Hawaii Volcanoes National Park, and on Kauai in the lowlands around Lihue. It's not known whether they can successfully reestablish themselves in the wild, because the introduced animals that prey on them haven't been controlled.

Nene "honk" like other geese, but you're more likely to hear another of their calls, a cow-like "moo." Here at Haleakala, they are filling a sort of ecological niche, but in their own *nene* style. On the mainland, the campground beggars are typically ground squirrels, bluejays, and raccoons—the latter two are out-and-out thieves. Haleakala's *nene* aren't thieves, but they're accomplished beggars. If you find them hanging around the cabins and campgrounds in the crater, look out! They'll come running for a handout when you unzip your daypack or pull some trail mix out of your pocket. You must be hardhearted and not feed them. (It's both the law and common sense, so they won't become dependent on people supplying food.) However, you will probably feel as guilty as I do when one of them stands there in front of you, eyeing your sandwich hopefully and mooing as if to say, "I'm endangered, I'm adorable, feed me!" Just hang onto your goodies. You'll be off the hook just as soon as someone else unzips a daypack or pulls out some trail mix!

Trip H4

Halemauu Trail to Holua Cabin

Dayhike or Backpack

Distance	Elevation gain	Hiking time	Topos
Just under 8 miles	1470' (Loss/gain)	4–6 hours	Kilohana 7½'

Difficulty: *Strenuous, hiking boots strongly recommended*

Highlights: *The awesome view from the Halemauu Trail at the crater rim, which is the destination of Trips H2 and H3, is just the beginning of this breathtaking scenic adventure down into the northwest corner of Haleakala's crater. This trail is so beautiful and so well-engineered that the return trip uphill can be as enjoyable as the descent if you take the*

*time to appreciate it. While it's described below as a dayhike, you can
also do it as a backpack if you can get permission to stay at Holua Cabin
or the adjacent campground.*

Driving instructions: Follow the driving instructions of Trip H3.

Permit/permission required: None for a dayhike. Required for
an overnight stay at Holua Cabin (by reservation only) or at the adjacent campground; see Appendix A.

Description: Follow Trip H3 to the crater rim and take in the view.
Now continue your zigzagging way down the Halemauu Trail, sometimes indistinct here because of multiple crossing tracks. Watch your

Crater near the Bottomless Pit

step if it's been raining, as these rocks can be very slippery. It's not long before you cross a narrow saddle where, if the cloud-cover permits, you have dizzying views into the crater on your right and down Haleakala's green northern slopes to the sea on your left—one of the very best viewpoints on this or any other hike in this book!

Soon you're negotiating carefully engineered switchbacks as you descend Leleiwi Pali to the crater floor. The grade is moderate to gentle, and the views are always spectacular. Stop often to enjoy them! One long switchback carries you around the other side of this ridge for a look down Koolau Gap. Seep springs dampen the black rock of the *pali*, which provides a perfect backdrop for the jewellike colors of the *amauu* fern.

You reach the crater floor at a stock gate in a little less than 3 miles from your start. Pass through the fence and please close the gate behind you. You may have expected to be on a dry, cinder-covered crater floor like the ones you see in most photographs of the crater. But here, the crater floor is a broad meadow of tall, waving grasses, nourished by the moisture in the clouds that flow through Koolau Gap. The trail is sometimes hard to see in the high growth, so watch your step and beware of half-hidden rocks. Bizarre, twisted peaks of half-vegetated lava rock rise out of the meadow here and there.

Holua Cabin sits atop a plateau on the opposite (south) side of this meadow. Follow the trail across the meadow, on the other side of which the trail rises gradually up the lava plateau in a few lazy switchbacks. You reach a T-junction atop the plateau, just under 4 miles from your start. The Halemauu Trail turns sharply left (southeast) here toward the Silversword Loop, Kawilinau (formerly "the Bottomless Pit"; the park wants to restore Hawaiian names to all named features wherever possible), and Paliku Cabin. You turn right to Holua Cabin, which is just a few steps away, sitting on a tidy, grassy flat. There's water, a picnic table, a toilet, and a few semi-resident *nene* here. If you're staying the night in the campground, it's 120 feet farther up the plateau on a short, steep spur trail that goes off to the left, past the water tap, as you face the cabin.

Return the way you came.

Hiker on trail near the Bottomless Pit

Amauu ferns

Amauu Fern

Mature *amauu* fronds are a bright green, while young fronds are a bright red. Together, set against the black rock, they're a sight you'll never forget. The red pigment is said to protect young fronds against the intense radiation at these altitudes.

Crater trails

The system of maintained trails leading down into and through the crater follows routes through this delicate ecosystem that are safe for you and for the environment. Going off the maintained trails can be physically hazardous and can damage the ecosystem, particularly in the extremely sensitive western part of the crater. Please don't step off the trail even to photograph the silverswords. You could be trampling and killing tiny silversword sprouts you can't even see. You'll find silverswords growing right next to the trail in several places, especially on the spur trail to Ka Lua o Ka Oo (Trip H12), so stepping off the trail is unnecessary. There aren't as many maintained trails as there used to be, "thanks" to cuts in the funding for national parks. But trust me on this: there's more than enough to explore on the remaining maintained trails to keep you busy for the few days you're permitted to spend in the crater. Haleakala National Park hopes to start maintaining more trails and to reopen closed ones over the next few years. Stick to the maintained trails, spare the environment, spare yourself injury, and help keep Haleakala beautiful.

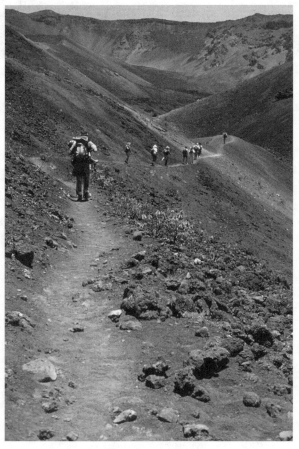

Hikers going away from Bottomless Pit

Trip H5

Holua Cabin/Campground
Side Trip to Kapalaoa Cabin

Distance	Elevation gain	Hiking time	Topos
Just under 6 miles	680'	3 hours	Kilohana 7½', Nahiku 7½'

Difficulty: *Strenuous, hiking boots strongly recommended*

Highlights: *This delightful semiloop takes you to the famous Silversword Loop and through some of the most colorful volcanic areas in the crater. It's one of several dayhikes you might take while staying at Holua Cabin/Campground. See the note at the end of Trip H2 for more ideas on crater dayhikes and backpacks.*

Driving instructions: Not applicable.

Permit/permission required: None for the side trip, which is a dayhike. Required to stay at Holua Cabin or the adjacent campground (see Trip H4 and Appendix A).

Description: Trip H4 has gotten you to Holua Cabin. This trip starts from the T-junction in front of Holua Cabin and bears southeast on the Halemauu Trail. You ascend gradually past a pit that is the open mouth of a lava tube and then through low ridges of jagged brown lava whose outcrops are crusted with a white lichen and whose protected hollows hold plants. At first you'll see *mamane, aalii,* sword ferns, and bracken ferns.

But soon the terrain becomes drier, and *ohelo, pilo, pukiawe, kukae-nene,* dubautias, and even a few silverswords appear. Lava cinders crunch under your boots. On either side of the trail, islands of fantastically shaped lava twist and twirl up from beds of black and red cinder. Sometimes the clouds from Koolau Gap drift in, leaving you alone in a misty world of goblin forms. At other times, you can see far across the crater to the cliffs enclosing it and to the red, brown, and black cinder cones that dot its floor. Pause often to look around you. It's one of earth's most striking landscapes, often referred to as a moonscape.

One mile from Holua, you reach the first of two junctions with the famous Silversword Loop. It's less a loop than a ¼-mile diversion from the Halemauu Trail. Veer left onto the Silversword Loop at this first junction for just over ¼ mile and then rejoin the main trail. When you've been around the Silversword Loop and come back to the Halemauu Trail, turn left to continue south on this dayhike.

Back on the Halemauu Trail, you descend briefly on soft, fine sand and walk through a red-tinged Mars-scape of bizarre lava rocks. Cinder cones rise on either side of the trail, and you soon reach another junction, just under 2 miles from your start at Holua Cabin/Campground. Both the left and the right forks here will get you to Kapalaoa Cabin and the Sliding Sands Trail, but take the left fork east toward Kawilinau (formerly "the Bottomless Pit") for now.

As you approach Kawilinau, you see a natural, if somewhat sloppy, bull's-eye of soft reds, grays, golds, and oranges ahead on the southeast slope of an unnamed cone. The slopes are a deep red with dots of fiery red and a brilliant splash of gold and orange at the saddle with Halalii cone. Orange, red, and lavender along the trail contrast with the dark

Sloppy bull's-eye in Pele's Paint Pot

brown slopes to your left, while on your right, pinks, golds, and reds spill into Halalii cone's vent. A lively brick red splashes up one slope, vivid orange another; nearby, there's a pit of shattered gray and red-brown rock. Grasses and dubautia make their homes here, adding a dash of green.

Now you know why this area is referred to as "Pele's Paint Pot." No subdued watercolors here—these are bold tempera colors, the result of minerals in the volcanic rock. Sulfur compounds are responsible for the yellows, iron for the reds. Fenced-off Kawilinau is not bottomless; according to a sign, it's 65 feet deep. Its depth may be forgettable, but its colors are memorable: pinks and reds burst from its throat; golds and grays tint its edges.

Ignore the unmarked side trail that leads south away from Kawilinau (it's just a shortcut over the saddle between Halalii and Puu

Trip H4
Start/end Trip H5

HALEAKALA

NATIONAL

PARK

N

Holua
Cabin/Campground

HALEMAUU TRAIL

SILVERSWORD LOOP

HALEMAUU TRAIL

Kawilinau
(formerly
"Bottomless Pit")

"Pele's Pig Pen"

Halalii

Ka Moa o Pele

"westernmost Sliding Sands-
Halemauu spur trail"

"middle Sliding Sands-
Halemauu spur trail"

BM x 7515

Puu o
Pele

SLIDING SANDS TRAIL

Trip H5 continues next page

0   1/4   1/2   1 mile

Naue to the trail you'll be returning on). Instead, continue generally eastward around Puu Naue, past brown-black cinder cones whose slopes are daubed with patches of orange and red. Ahead looms Puu Mamane, its northern slopes green with vegetation, its southern slopes bare red cinders.

Now you pass through a cinder-strewn landscape as desolate as any you've seen; silverswords grow high on the slopes to your right. Soon, the bare, reddish cone of Puu Nole rises ahead on your right, Puu Mamane on your left. You pass a couple of use trails down which you have views of Kapalaoa Cabin.

At the next marked junction, on a cinder flat between Puu Mamane and Puu Nole, you turn hard right, initially south-southwest but then generally south-southeast toward Kapalaoa Cabin on the easternmost Sliding Sands-Halemauu spur trail. This junction is almost halfway between Holua and Paliku. The green-clad *pali* behind the

Lava bombs

cabin dominate the scenery as you begin a descent between Puu Naue and Puu Nole. As you approach the red slopes of another cone, you see that they have a sparse cover of bracken fern and silversword. A group of silverswords grows where the trail brushes past a ridge extending from the cone. Jagged chunks of rock protrude through the sand here, looking like the spine of a prehistoric monster half-buried in the sand.

You level out on black sand that's tinged with lavender and strewn with red and orange cinders; soon you reach a junction with the Sliding Sands Trail. Turn left (east) here for a few steps to Kapalaoa Cabin, 1¼ mile from Kawilinau. Here you'll find a toilet, a picnic table, water, and *nene* anxious to help you polish off that granola bar. There's no tent-campground here: water at Kapalaoa Cabin is limited to precipitation collected from the roof, and there's not enough to support both a cabin and a campground.

The trail that goes north immediately in front of Kapalaoa Cabin is not a maintained trail, so you go west ⅓ mile, past the junction with the trail you descended on, to the next marked trail junction. Turn right (northwest) here onto the middle Sliding Sands-Halemauu spur trail toward Holua Cabin.

You head toward Puu Naue through bunches of a native alpine tussock grass—a sort of meadow and just about the last thing you'd expect to see in this lava wilderness. The grass ends as you pass a red-cinder hillock, and you traverse a region of black and reddish sand and of lava frozen as it oozed across the landscape. The rocks here are riddled with holes left by gas bubbles and brushed with subtle hues from cream through orange, red, and black.

You cross a spine of lava, climb past a miniature butte of red rock, and level out amid reddish cinders and black boulders. A remnant of a *pahoehoe* flow, markedly smoother than the *aa* you've been passing, appears on your left. The trail is plain ahead of you, winding up to the saddle between Ka Moa o Pele and Halalii cones. Ka Moa o Pele's huge red vent gapes at you, its edges dusted with ochre and gray. You pass more *pahoehoe*, cross a stretch of black cinders, and abruptly enter a region of light-colored cinders—white, tan, pink-orange—on which sit isolated lava bombs.

The light-colored cinders end as abruptly as they began, and you're soon on the saddle between Ka Moa o Pele and Halalii cones at the junction with the spur trail around Halalii, a little under 1 mile from Kapalaoa Cabin. Head northwest (right) past a little, squarish vent called "Pele's Pig Pen" to the junction where, earlier, you turned off to Kawilinau.

Bear left (northwest) on the Halemauu Trail here and retrace your steps to Holua Cabin to end this beautiful dayhike.

Trip H6

Halemauu Trail to Paliku Cabin/Campground
Backpack

Distance	Elevation gain	Hiking time	Topos
2⅔ miles	2690' (Loss/gain)	15–16 hours (over 3 days)	Kilohana 7½', Nahiku 7½'

Difficulty: *Strenuous, hiking boots strongly recommended*

Highlights: *The soft, green beauty of the pali and meadows near Holua Cabin/Campground and around Paliku Cabin/Campground contrast marvelously with the vivid mineral colors and harsh aridity of the crater backcountry that separates them.*

Driving instructions: Follow the driving instructions of Trip H3.

Permit/permission required: Haleakala National Park permit required to stay overnight at Holua Cabin/Campground or Paliku Cabin/Campground or both. See "Getting Permits or Permission" on page 6 and Appendix A.

Description: You can organize this trip in a number of different ways depending on the permits you're able to get and whether you want to take a layover day. Clearly, going all the way to Paliku in one day and all the way out in one day is the most strenuous version. I've described an easier version below: you go all the way to Paliku in one day—mostly downhill—and take two days to walk out, staying one night at Holua Cabin/Campground.

Trip H6 continues next page

Continue Trip H6

Trip H4

Start/end Trip H5

N

HALEAKALA

NATIONAL

PARK

Holua
Cabin/Campground

HALEMAUU TRAIL

SILVERSWORD LOOP

HALEMAUU TRAIL

Kawilinau
(formerly
"Bottomless Pit")

"Pele's Pig Pen"

Halalii

Continue Trip H6 next page

| 0 | 1/4 | 1/2 | 1 mile |

Day 1 (10½ miles): Follow Trip H4 to Holua Cabin/Campground. From there, follow Trip H5 to the marked junction between Puu Mamane and Puu Nole, where Trip H5 turns hard right toward Kapalaoa Cabin. Bear left (ahead; east) along the north slope of Puu Nole and toward Paliku Cabin/Campground at that junction. After descending the north slope of Namana o ke Akua, you presently reach a saddle where a low, vegetated hill, Oili Puu, rises ahead of you. As you continue down, north of Honokahua, on a couple of long switch-back legs, the cliffs around the crater begin to assume a softer, greener look. Soon you're grazing across an almost-African looking landscape, where the *veldt* is shrubs and bracken rather than grass, dotted by green

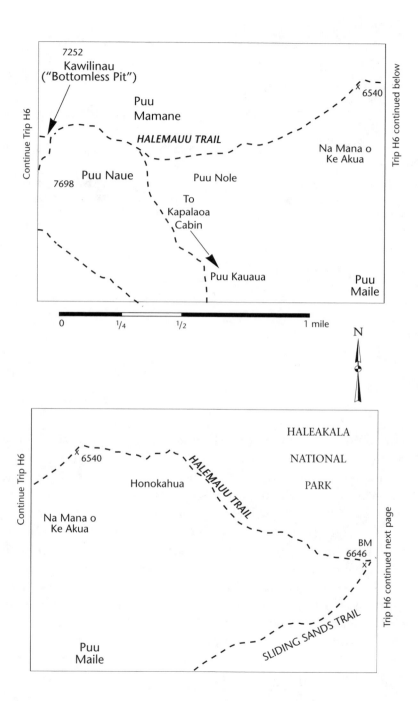

7252
Kawilinau
("Bottomless Pit")

Puu
Mamane

HALEMAUU TRAIL

6540

Na Mana o
Ke Akua

Continue Trip H6

Trip H6 continued below

Puu Naue

7698

Puu Nole

To
Kapalaoa
Cabin

Puu Kauaua

Puu
Maile

0   ¼   ½   1 mile

N

6540

HALEAKALA

NATIONAL

PARK

Honokahua

HALEMAUU TRAIL

Na Mana o
Ke Akua

BM
6646

Continue Trip H6

Trip H6 continued next page

SLIDING SANDS TRAIL

Puu
Maile

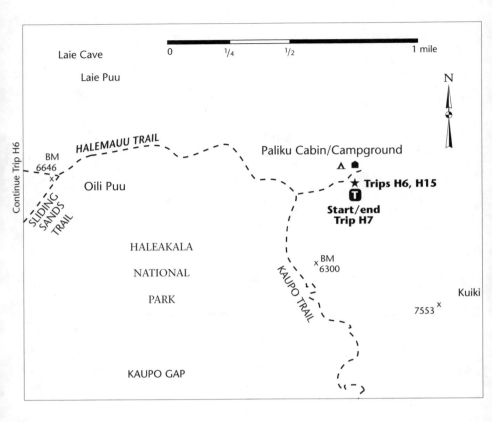

kopjes whose tops sport tree-sized *mamane* rather than the airy African acacia. You descend gradually onto the veldt, and you presently see what looks like a dry wash ahead. The trail leads down to it. In some places, the trail is right in the wash; in others, where the bottom of the wash is very rocky, the trail leads you around its edges.

At the foot of shrub-covered Oili Puu, you reach the junction of the Halemauu and Sliding Sands trails. Turn left (northeast) here toward Paliku Cabin/Campground, abandoning the wash and following a path sometimes over *pahoehoe* and sometimes worn deeply through the shrub-and-bracken plain. The troughs of the grey-black *pahoehoe* ripples are sometimes highlighted by a delicate trace of red color. At a junction with the trail heading down Kaupo Gap, you can just glimpse Paliku Cabin to the northeast. It's surrounded by trees and nestled at the foot of a lushly green *pali*, sometimes framed in a rainbow by late-afternoon light refracted through a fine rain. Bear left (northeast) on the side trail ¼ mile to Paliku Cabin/Campground, 6⅓ miles from Holua Cabin/Campground. At a fork, the right one leads to a ranger's cabin; you go left toward the hiker's cabin and campground. The spur trail to the campground is on your left a few dozen yards before you get to Paliku Cabin. *Nene* may patrol the picnic area in front of the cabin and the adjacent campground, mooing for a handout. The pit toilet is uphill on a trail behind the cabin. Not far from Paliku cabin, there's a rangers' cabin (almost hidden) and a meadow where horses graze. It's a lovely place to stay, and you'll probably want to spend two nights here in order to take Trip H7.

Day 2 (6⅓ miles): Reverse your steps from Paliku Cabin/Campground to Holua Cabin/Campground.

Day 3 (Just under 4 miles): Reverse your steps from Holua Cabin/Campground to the Halemauu trailhead.

Paliku Cabin

Why the great variations in the amount of vegetation?

You'll no doubt have noticed the great variation in the amount of vegetation in the crater.
What a contrast the arid volcanic landscapes around
the Silversword Loop and Kawilinau make with
the meadows around Holua Cabin/Campground
and Paliku Cabin/Campground! One factor is the difference in precipitation the different parts of the crater receive. In general, the crater
floor near Koolau Gap (Holua Cabin/Campground and the meadow)
shares the moisture of East Maui's rainy northern coast, which flows
through Koolau Gap. The crater floor here is just within the inversion-
layer zone. Above Paliku Cabin/Campground, there's a notch in the
slim ridge still separating Kipahulu Valley from Kaupo Gap and
Haleakala's crater. Moisture from the very wet Hana-Kipahulu coast
pours through this notch, nourishing Paliku. By contrast, the southwest edge of the crater is on the dry, leeward side of the island and is
high above the inversion-layer zone. Annual rainfall in the crater varies
from 20 inches there to 200 or more inches at Paliku!

But rainfall variations alone aren't enough to explain the differ-
ences. An annual rainfall of 20 inches a year is more than enough to
sustain a cover of vegetation in many areas of the world. However, in
order for that vegetation to flourish, the soil must retain the water it
receives. The crater's cinder cones, remnants of its last phase of volcanic
activity, have made the crater both a visual delight and an inhospitable
desert. Their eruptions covered most of the crater with a porous layer
of cinder and ash, reported to be 3000 feet deep in some places. That
layer allows whatever precipitation falls to percolate right through it.
Little water is retained, except in isolated pockets, to feed plants. Nooks
like Paliku escaped those cinders. Unlike the cinder deserts, their older,
more-consolidated soils retain life-giving water and create these green
oases.

Trip H7

Paliku Cabin/Campground
Side Trip to Park Boundary

Distance	Elevation gain	Hiking time	Topos
8 miles	2560' (Loss/gain)	4 hours	Nahiku 7½', Kaupo 7½'

Difficulty: Strenuous, hiking boots strongly recommended

Highlights: A fascinating descent through scrubland, forest, and meadow, with fine views downslope to the coast around Kaupo village. This trip complements Trip E14.

Driving instructions: Not applicable.

Trip H7 continues next page

Permit/permission required: None just for this side trip, but you must have permission to stay in the crater as described in Trips H4 and H6.

Description: Trip H6 or H15 brought you to Paliku Cabin/Campground. To begin this trip, retrace your steps from Paliku Cabin/Campground to the junction with the trail that goes down Kaupo Gap. Turn left (southwest) toward the dark peak, Haleakala, that guards the west side of Kaupo Gap. (Haleakala peak is too far south and west of the trail to appear on the book's maps.) Opposite, Kuiki peak watches Kaupo Gap's east side. The trail presently veers south and begins a descent on a cindery surface through the scrub you've come to recognize as typical of this region. Look for some almost-tree-sized *iaali* shrubs here. In ½ mile from Paliku, you begin a series of cinder-covered switchbacks. White-flowered *ulei* grows here, as do many splendid

Haleakala Peak, Kaupo Gap

amauu ferns. Down you go, leveling out in a little forest, then emerging into a meadow of waving grasses through which you follow the trail to the edge of this bench. Here, you may be startled to realize that the blue vastness ahead of you is only half sky. The lower portion is the sparkling ocean, so far away that it blends into the sky.

You switchback briefly down to another bench and another meadow. From here, you make a delightful descent over an old, built-up trail whose supporting lava-rock walls are covered with a thick white fluff of lichens. Spikes of small, blue-flowered vervain sway along the trailside. Now you reach a third bench, pushing your way first through blackberry and then through dense grass. The sheer walls of Kaupo Gap loom high on your left.

Rounding a curve, you find yourself walking south along the west side of a gully whose shady east side is well-clothed in native plants, including *ohia* trees, *amauu* ferns, and *mamane* shrubs. As you veer west and then south, the view opens up again, and you see some fine *koa* trees down in the gully. On the rocks to your right, look for the low, trailing *kukaenene* with its shiny black berries.

The next series of switchbacks offers breathtaking views down to Kaupo and the sea, west to Haleakala peak, and back up to the misty *pali.* The trail becomes very rocky, and with so many loose rocks, it's wise to pause when you want to enjoy the scenery. You leave the rocks at a little clearing in the now-predominant *koa.* The terrain has become drier as you have descended, as you can see from the shrubbier forms of the *mamane* and *pukiawe.* Soon the trail becomes rocky again, and you resume descending on switchbacks under the shade of *koa* trees. At a little emerald meadow, pause to check the gentle slope ahead and slightly to your right (south-southwest) to see where the trail resumes, as it all but vanishes in the lush grass here. Make your way across the meadow and pick up the trail again as it rises briefly on the low ridge, then follows the ridge generally south through scrub, becoming quite rocky and sometimes steep. Soon you begin a series of grassy switch-backs that bring you to the protective fence of the Kaupo Gap Study Area.

Now you descend moderately on a track that's more often grass than rock. The slopes ahead of you frame distant, square-shaped Kamanawa Bay west of Kaupo village. At an apparent fork, either fork will do, but watch your footing on the deep grass. It makes a spongy surface to walk on and conceals some loose rocks. You pass a National Park boundary sign on the other side of which is a sign announcing that you're now on Kaupo Ranch's private property. Soon you cross a gully above some *koa* trees and, as the track grows faint, duck into a lovely grove of *koa* just before the park's protective boundary fence. Remember that if you do go through the fence, you must be sure the gate shuts securely behind you, even if you have to trample the grass down to make it close.

Retrace your steps to Paliku Cabin/Campground when you're ready. (To continue to Kaupo, reverse the steps of Trip E14.)

Maui and Haleakala peak

Shelters, platforms, and a *heiau* are said to be located on Haleakala peak, signs that it once had religious significance. One source speculates that Haleakala peak may be the site of the demigod Maui's mythical encounter with La, the sun. There are many versions of this myth, but all agree that long ago, the lazy sun moved across the sky so quickly that the day was very short. La arose from his resting-place reluctantly, hurried as fast as he could through his work of lighting and warming the earth, and rushed home to his leisure without a thought for the long nights that people had to endure. The day was far too short for Maui's mother, the goddess Hina, to dry her *kapa*, the bark cloth characteristic of Polynesia. Hina asked Maui to find a way to dry her *kapa*.

Here on Hale-a-ka-La, the House of the Sun, Maui prepared ropes and hid so he could surprise La as he rose, climbing over the walls of Haleakala crater like a spider, one leg—ray—at a time. As La put each leg over the *pali*, Maui lassoed it. He held La captive until La promised to move across the sky more slowly. Even then, some accounts say, Maui left a few of the ropes on La's legs. You can see them trailing off into the sky just before the sun sets.

The island of Maui is unique in Polynesia: it is the only island named for a deity. Maui was a great mischief-maker, and legends about his escapades (or "strifes") occur throughout Polynesia. Martha Beckwith reported in *Hawaiian Mythology* that Maui legends in Hawaii tend to be "minutely localized." East Maui, West Maui, the Big Island of Hawaii, Oahu, and Kauai all have their own versions of the same Maui exploit, placing the exploit's location somewhere on that island. For East Maui, Maui's tricks usually occur near Kauiki at Hana; for West Maui, near Kahakuloa. Haleakala isn't one of the sites Dr. Beckwith records in association with Maui's legends. Still, legends are fluid, and Haleakala certainly seems appropriate as a poetic, if not entirely traditional, site for Maui's capture of La.

Trip H8

Leleiwi Pali Overlook Mini-hike

Distance	Elevation gain	Hiking time	Topos
Less than ⅓ mile	Negligible	9 minutes	Kilohana 7½' (Optional)

Difficulty: *Easy, tennis shoes recommended*

Highlights: *Interpretive signs make this tiny trail especially interesting as you make your way to a shelter high atop the cliffs of Leleiwi Pali, where the view into Haleakala's "crater" is simply breathtaking, weather permitting.*

Driving instructions: From Hosmer Grove, continue 8 more miles up the highway. Here you'll find a small parking lot on the uphill side of the road.

Permit/permission required: None.

Description: Take the crosswalk across the highway to the signed start of the hiking trail and descend briefly northeast to reach the first of the interpretive signs. Shortly the trail begins to curve generally east on a gradual ascent. Fine views open up downslope, clouds permitting. Native plants you'll see along the way include bracken fern, *mamane* with is pea-like yellow flowers, needle-leafed *pukiawe*, the orange-berried pilo, and the yellow-flowered dubautia (*kupaoa*), which is so closely related to the silversword that it can hybridize with the latter.

As the trail nears its end at a sheltered overlook, there are astonishing views of the crater, including the Halemauu Trail snaking down the cliffs and across the meadows hundreds of feet below, the rugged Leleiwi Pali falling away just below your feet, the Koolau Gap on your left, and, far across the crater, the Kaupo Gap. By afternoon, clouds may be silently creeping up from the not-so-distant ocean through both gaps—a lovely sight to watch as they gradually obscure your view and fill the crater.

Retrace your steps to the parking lot when you can tear yourself away from this splendid view.

Trip H9

Kalahaku Overlook Mini-loop

Distance	Elevation gain	Hiking time	Topos
⅕ mile	40'	Less than 10 minutes	Kilohana 7½' (Optional)

Difficulty: *Very easy, tennis shoes recommended*

Highlights: *This brief trip offers fine crater views and a visit to a little garden of silverswords in just a few brief minutes of walking with little elevation gain. Non-hikers, this is the Haleakala trip for you!*

Driving instructions: Follow the driving instructions of Trip H4 past the Halemauu Trail turnoff. Continue up the highway to the Visitor Center at White Hill, 40⅓ miles from Wailuku, *deliberately driving past the turnoff for the Kalahaku Overlook*—all but invisible when driving up the highway. You're not allowed to turn off here when you're going uphill. Turn around in the parking lot at the Visitor Center and drive back down the highway just over 1½ miles to the turnoff for the Kalahaku Overlook, well-marked for downhill traffic. Turn right here and follow the spur road to the farther of two small parking areas, 42 miles from Wailuku. (It's 38¾ miles from Wailuku plus the slightly over 3 miles you drove to the Visitor Center and back.)

Permit/permission required: None.

Description: Near the end of the spur road, a paved path leads up to an overlook shelter. Taking this path, you climb with the help of some stairs past a sign explaining the impact non-native animals have had on native plants and animals. Don't take the path that branches to the right at a junction here; instead, continue ahead to the shelter on the crater rim. There's a magnificent crater view from the shelter, and interpretive signs explain the many crater cones you can see below to the east and southeast. To the west, you can see West Maui.

It's hard to leave this view, but when you're ready, retrace your steps to the exotic-animal sign. Turn left at the junction here and follow the paved path down a gentle descent with a short flight of stairs

Haleakala Crater

to the road. Cross the road and descend the stairs that are just a little to your right. Turn left at the bottom of the stairs and follow the paved path along the silversword viewing area. You can't walk out into the silversword garden, but you can walk back and forth here to see how the light brings out the silvery patina on these remarkable plants. The number of silverswords varies—they don't live forever—so cross your fingers that there'll be lots when you're here.

The path winds back up to the road, where you turn left (north) and retrace your steps back to your car.

The Brocken specter

The Brocken specter is a natural light show in which you are both audience and star: your shadow on a cloud bank below you, surrounded by a rainbow ring. It's often seen at Haleakala, particularly from Leleiwi Pali (for example, Leleiwi Overlook, just down the highway). Afternoon sunlight behind you casts your shadow onto the clouds drifting through Koolau Gap. The light around your shadow is reflected back from the cloud by

243

the water droplets that make it up. Like tiny prisms, these water drop-lets also refract the light into the familiar colors of the rainbow. You see the rainbow effect as a colored halo around your shadow.

You don't believe that's your shadow? Wave your arms and watch the shadow follow suit. Worldwide, seeing the Brocken specter used to be rare; nowadays, airline passengers frequently see the Brocken specter from the airplane. Still, it's much more exciting when the rainbow-cir-cled shadow is yours, not the airplane's! The phenomenon is named for Brocken Mountain in Germany, where it was first described.

White Hill Visitor Center

Trip H10

White Hill

Distance	Elevation gain	Hiking time	Topos
Less than ½ mile	140'	15 minutes	Kilohana 7½'

Difficulty: *Easy, tennis shoes recommended*

Highlights: *The awesome panorama from the top of White Hill is something you won't forget. White Hill's summit is one of the favored places for watching sunrise at Haleakala, too. So is the Visitor Center, but it's usually crowded with those who came unprepared to wait in the icy dark. The vigil demands plenty of warm, windproof clothing—don't forget that warm hat and those gloves or mittens, either.*

Driving instructions: Follow the driving instructions of Trip H3 past the Halemauu Trail turnoff and continue up the highway to the Visitor Center at White Hill, 40⅓ miles from Wailuku.

Permit/permission required: None.

Description: The trail up White Hill begins near the Visitor Center building, to its right as you face the building from the parking lot. It's a gentle but rocky grade; if you're coming here in the frigid predawn darkness, you'll need a flashlight to keep yourself on the trail and to avoid tripping over the rocks. The trail winds almost 360° around the hill as it rises to the summit, where a few tough dubautias live. From here, you have superb views in all directions once it's light. To the southwest sits Haleakala's high point, Red Hill (Trip H18). Southeast, you look over the crater walls to the summits of Mauna Kea and Mauna Loa on the Big Island of Hawaii, many miles away across the ocean. To the west, you have amazing views of the Isthmus and West Maui. And below you to the east, steep cliffs fall away into the crater. Perhaps the crater is clear of mist and dramatic with its cinder cones and sheer walls, or perhaps it's filled with clouds through which the cones push their dark heads. Nothing but the thin air separates you from the crater, making you feel almost as if you had wings and were soaring high above it.

It's hard to retrace your steps from here. After you've done so, but before you leave, stop in at the Visitor Center to enjoy the exhibits, browse for another book, and get your questions answered by the ranger on duty.

Trip H11

Sliding Sands Trail to "Rock Garden"

Distance	Elevation gain	Hiking time	Topos
2 miles	560' (Loss/gain)	1 hour	Kilohana 7½'

Difficulty: *Moderate, tennis shoes recommended*

Highlights: *This relatively short descent on the famous Sliding Sands Trail offers you a chance to experience hiking in Haleakala's crater and to enjoy some wonderful crater views.*

Driving instructions: Follow the driving instructions of Trip H10. The Sliding Sands Trail is on the side of the parking lot nearer the highway (away from the Visitor Center building).

Permit/permission required: None.

Description: Pause at the trailhead sign to read its information and to pick up one of the park's brochures on hiking trails. Now that you're fully informed, follow the path away from the parking lot, briefly paralleling the highway. You're at the crater rim in a little over ⅛ mile. You can't help but pause and think, *How vast and lifeless the crater seems from here!* Ahead, the Sliding Sands Trail stretches away along the cindery crater wall, dwindling till it seems little more than a scratch in the dark sand. Specks moving on the distant scratch will turn out to be your fellow hikers. Down in the crater, clouds drift in and out among the brown and red hulks of distant cinder cones, constantly changing the view. Far, far away at the east end of the crater, Kaupo Gap breaks the stark crater walls, mists ebbing and flowing through it. Perhaps you had thought you could easily orient yourself here; now, the crater's immensity may seem almost intimidating and its shifting clouds may defy your attempts to positively identify the landmarks that seemed so obvious from the Visitor Center.

The well-graded trail is pleasant walking, and you're soon descending, negotiating a couple of switchbacks, and looking forward to your next photo stop. You presently drop into the shallow depression between a low ridge on your left and the crater wall. At the next switchback, just under 1 mile from your start, you come upon a handsome formation of red-brown rock around which grow a number of bright green shrubs with cheery little puffs of yellow flowers. This striking natural arrangement

Sliding Sands trailhead

of forms and colors is what I've called the "rock garden." These are dubautias, specifically _Dubautia menziesii,_ one of the plants most characteristic of this arid landscape (more about them below). Other dubautias grow in and around Haleakala, but this particular one, with its small, stiff, succulent leaves arranged rather formally in fours, is especially conspicuous because it seeks no shelter, growing instead in the most exposed places. A few stunted _pukiawe,_ another hardy native shrub, grow here, too, but the dubautias are really the show.

When you're ready, retrace your steps.

Dubautias and their relatives

Botanists believe that the endemic dubautias (_Dubautia_) and their showier endemic relatives, the silverswords (_Argyroxiphium_) and _iliau_ (_Wilkesia_), share a common ancestor with the present-day tarweeds of California. The common California tarweed is a daisy-like annual plant, not particularly showy, competing with many other mainland species for survival and having few opportunities to radiate into different environmental niches.

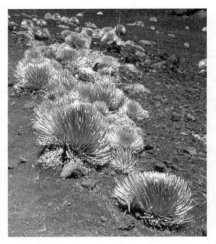

Silversword

The tarweeds that reached Hawaii, probably as bristly seeds stuck to birds' feathers, have undergone one of the most amazing adaptive radiations to be found in the Hawaiian Islands. As their common ancestor was adapted to dry locations, it's not surprising to find dubautias, silverswords, and *iliau* in arid places. But many dubautias have evolved into shrubs and trees of the rainforests. One dubautia even grows on the summit of Kauai's Mt. Waialeale, possibly the rainiest spot on earth. Another rare dubautia is a vine in Kauai's *koa* forests.

The Haleakala silversword occupies the extremely arid, bright alpine environment. The Kau silversword grows in a moist region on the slopes of Mauna Loa on the Big Island of Hawaii. More amazing still are the silverswords and greenswords (like silverswords but lacking silvery hairs) that grow in bogs like the one on Puu Kukui, the highest point on West Maui and another of the rainiest spots on earth.

The shrubby dubautias and the rosette-shaped silverswords are so closely related that they can hybridize naturally. *Plants and Flowers of Hawai'i* includes a photograph of one such natural hybrid, between the *Dubautia menziesii* you see here at the "rock garden" and the Haleakala silversword, *Argyroxiphium sandwicense*.

The *iliau*, one of only two members of its genus, occupies a moderately dry, scrubby forest niche around Waimea Canyon on Kauai. It's rare, but it doesn't seem to be an endangered species.

Apparently, the only major environmental niche the dubautia-silversword-*iliau* family doesn't occupy in the Hawaiian Islands is the lower coastal region—but it's one of the principal niches occupied by their California tarweed relatives and their presumed common ancestor. Perhaps that niche was already fully occupied when the ancestor of the dubautia-silversword-*iliau* family arrived, so the adaptable family went on to evolve into forms that occupy virtually every other niche in Hawaii.

Trip H12

Sliding Sands Trail to Ka Lua o Ka Oo

To Wailuku • Makawao
Pukalani (377)
N
(37)
Waiakoa (378)
Park HQ
To Hwy. 31, Keokea, Kaupo
Sliding Sands
Red Hill •

Distance	Elevation gain	Hiking time	Topos
4¾+ miles	1600' (Loss/gain)	2½–3 hours	Kilohana 7½'

Difficulty: *Strenuous, tennis shoes recommended*

Highlights: *Ka Lua o Ka Oo ("Kalua O Ka Oo" on the topo, "Ka Luu o ka Oo" on a park brochure) is one of the most colorful cones in the crater. The way it's tucked into the steep ridge below Red Hill means there's very little climbing required to get to its top. As a bonus, the spur trail from the Sliding Sands Trail to Ka Lua O Ka Oo presently has one of the best concentrations of silverswords to be found in the crater, several growing very near the trail, so there's no excuse or need for stepping off* *the trail to get your own silversword photograph. A park brochure may be available for this hike; check at the trailhead. It says that "Ka Luu o ka Oo" means "the plunge [luu] of the digging-stick [oo]."*

Driving instructions: Follow the driving instructions of Trip H10.

Permit/permission required: None.

Description: Follow the Sliding Sands Trail down to the "rock garden" as described in Trip H11. Continue down the ridge, where views of the crater open up again as you switchback away from the "rock garden." Silverswords appear along the trail as you approach the junction with the spur trail to Ka Lua o Ka Oo, a little over 1¾ miles. The junction is set amid jagged lava formations, and you turn left (north) here toward the cone.

The spur trail makes a short, steep, rough descent at first. Then it levels out and curves around the steep but shallow depression below Red Hill and White Hill, revealing a landscape of red-brown cinders enlivened by the shining gray-white of silversword rosettes and the sprightly green of dubautia shrubs. Climbing a little, the spur trail leads right to the edge of the cone, from which a use trail bears left around the cone's deep, brightly colored vent. Bluish-gray rocks dot the

Sliding Sands Trail

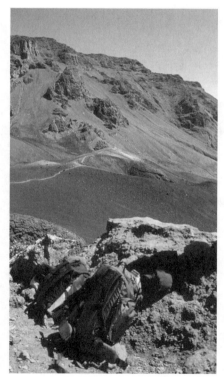

Backpacks and Ka Lua o Ka Oo

scene, and splashes of mineral colors stain the vent's throat and edges: reds, pinks, tans, blacks, oranges, golds, yellows, chocolates, and lavenders. Oh, for a wide-angle lens to capture all these wonderful colors at once!

As you enjoy this spectacle, Haleakala's clouds may drift in and drizzle on you, then float out, leaving the cone awash in sunlight, then swirl in again. Photography hint: in *Haleakala: A Guide to the Mountain*, the authors advise shutterbugs to meter off the ground, not off the too-bright sky, to avoid underexposures of crater scenery.

Too soon, it's time to return the way you came—almost all uphill now—to your car.

Trip H13

Sliding Sands to Kapalaoa Cabin
Dayhike or Backpack

To Wailuku • Makawao   N

Pukalani   (377)

(37)

Waiakoa   (378)

To   Park HQ
Hwy. 31,   □ **Sliding
Keokea,   Red Hill •   Sands**
Kaupo

Distance	Elevation gain	Hiking time	Topos
11½–13½ miles	2680' (Loss/gain)	7–8 hours	Kilohana 7½', Nahiku 7½'

Difficulty: *Strenuous, hiking boots strongly recommended*

Highlights: *All the visual delights of Trips H11 and H12, plus a visit to Kapalaoa Cabin's tiny oasis. Crater views on the way back from Kapalaoa Cabin are especially stunning. I've described this trip as a dayhike, but you can also do it as a backpack if you can get a reservation for Kapalaoa Cabin.*

Sliding Sands Trail

Driving instructions: Follow the driving instructions of Trip H10.

Permit/permission required: None for dayhike. Required for an overnight stay at Kapalaoa Cabin (by reservation only); see Appendix A. There is no campground at Kapalaoa Cabin, so it's the cabin or nothing.

Description: Follow Trip H12 to Ka Lua O Ka Oo, but on your return to the junction with the Sliding Sands Trail, turn left and continue east down the trail. You come around some rocks to see wonderful colors on the adjacent hillsides—pinks, reds, and lavenders. As Puu o Pele looms ahead, you pass through an area of silverswords and presently begin hiking over rocks—chunks of *aa*—instead of the cinders you've been on till now. This area, which appears to be a dull, dark, monochrome from above, reveals itself to be full of subtle colors and intriguing textures. The view back up the Sliding Sands Trail from here is very striking.

You bear east-southeast past heaps of brick-red cinder near the top of Puu o Pele, then zigzag down, down, down its sides to a junction with the westernmost spur trail going north to Holua Cabin/-Campground and the Halemauu Trail. There's a hitching rail here, along with a sad-looking *mamane* that serves as the local toilet. Dark-brown Puu o Maui, the highest cone in the crater, is off to the north on one side of the spur trail, reddish Ka Moa o Pele on the other. South of you, on the crater walls, there's a patch of bracken fern. When it turns orange-gold in the fall, you may wonder if you've stumbled upon a field of California poppies in bloom. Here, 4 miles from your start, you bear right (ahead) toward Kapalaoa Cabin.

An unexpected delight, an alpine meadow of bracken fern, evening primrose, and tussock grasses, with the occasional mamane and dubautia, grows along the Sliding Sands Trail between here and Kapalaoa Cabin. As you continue east, Ka Moa o Pele recedes, and you're able to see Halalii, Puu Naue, and Puu Nole cones to the north. You pass two more junctions with spur trails northward to Holua Cabin/Campground and the Halemauu Trail, but you persist eastward to Kapalaoa

Kawilinau
(formerly
"Bottomless Pit")

HALEMAUU TRAIL

HALEAKALA

NATIONAL

PARK

N

"Pele's Pig Pen"

Halalii

Ka Moa o Pele

BM x 7515

"westernmost Sliding Sands-Halemauu spur trail"

"middle Sliding Sands-Halemauu spur trail"

Puu o
Pele

SLIDING SANDS TRAIL

Continue Trip H13

Trip H13 continues below

0   1/4   1/2   1 mile

Kawilinau
("Bottomless Pit")

HALEMAUU TRAIL

Na Mana o Ke Akua

N

Puu Naue

Puu Nole

HALEAKALA

NATIONAL

PARK

7698

"easternmost Sliding Sands-Halemauu spur trail"

"middle Sliding Sands-Halemauu spur trail"

Puu Kauaua

Puu Maile

Start/end
Trip H14

Trip H5, H13

SLIDING SANDS TRAIL

Kapalaoa Cabin

Continue Trip H13

Cabin. The third junction is only ¹⁄₁₀ mile from Kapalaoa Cabin, which is perched on a small, grassy platform just south of the trail, dwarfed by the scrub-covered *pali* rising behind it. A picnic table, pit toilet, and water are available here, a little over 5¾ miles from your start (6¾ miles if you detoured to see Ka Lua o Ka Oo). It's a wonderful place to rest, enjoy your lunch, and take in the awesome crater views. Resist the temptation to share your lunch with the engaging and shameless *nene* beggars here!

Retrace your steps to White Hill when you must; be sure to allow plenty of time for the steep pull up the hill.

Did the old Hawaiians come up to Haleakala crater?

There's no evidence that anyone ever lived permanently high on Haleakala or down in its crater, but there are ruins of stone shelters that the old Hawaiians used for temporary shelter while they were up here. The Hawaiians found the necessities of life in the ocean, on the coastal plains, and on the lower mountain slopes, not in the alien harshness of this high mountain. Yet there's plenty of evidence that the upper slopes and crater of Haleakala were ceremonially and economically important. The note at the end of Trip H7 mentioned the *heiau* on Haleakala peak. A survey of Haleakala (Emory, 1921, reported by Kirch in *Feathered Gods and Fishhooks*) lists "[58] terraces and platforms . . ., [9] groups of open stone shelters, 'several hundred' cairns, and a section of an ancient paved road. . . . Several of the terraces and cairns proved to contain burials." Slingstones found on the crater floor suggest that the Hawaiians came up here to hunt birds. They also came to Haleakala to mine its outcrops of fine-grained basalt, which was an excellent material for making adzes (cutting tools used chiefly for shaping wood). Radiocarbon dating of charcoal from one of the stone shelters shows people were here perhaps as early as the eighth century. The ancient paved road, which once connected Wailuku and Hana but has almost disappeared now, may indicate that the Hawaiians preferred the arduous climb up and down Haleakala to the tortuous coastal routes.

Trip H14
Kapalaoa Cabin
Side Trip to Holua Cabin/Campground

Distance	Elevation gain	Hiking time	Topos
8⅔ miles	790′	4⅓ hours	Kilohana 7½′, Nahiku 7½

Difficulty: *Strenuous, hiking boots strongly recommended*

Highlights: *Many of the same scenic joys that highlight Trip H5 highlight this trip, too. However, this trip returns to Kapalaoa Cabin on the westernmost of the three maintained spur trails between the Sliding Sands and Halemauu trails. The return leg, passing between Puu o Maui and Ka Moa o Pele, offers a different experience of the crater floor from that offered by Trip H5.*

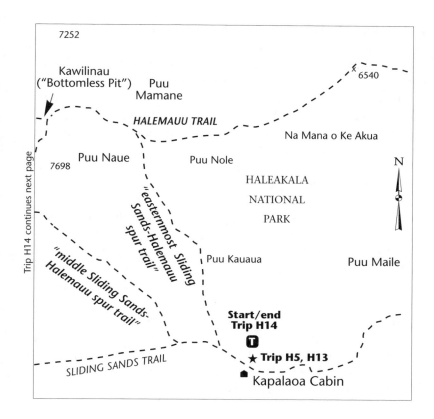

7252

Kawilinau
("Bottomless Pit")　Puu
Mamane

6540

HALEMAUU TRAIL

Na Mana o Ke Akua

Puu Naue
7698

Puu Nole

HALEAKALA

NATIONAL

PARK

N

"easternmost Sliding
Sands-Halemauu
spur trail"

Puu Kauaua

Puu Maile

"middle Sliding Sands-
Halemauu spur trail"

Start/end
Trip H14

T

★ Trip H5, H13

SLIDING SANDS TRAIL

Kapalaoa Cabin

Trip H14 continues next page

Driving instructions: Not applicable.

Permit/permission required: None for this dayhike. Required to stay at Kapalaoa Cabin (see Trip H13 and Appendix A).

Description: From Kapalaoa Cabin, retrace your steps ⅓ mile west to the junction with the middle (second) maintained spur trail linking the Sliding Sands and Halemauu trails, as described in Trip H5. Follow this spur trail northwest to the saddle between Ka Moa o Pele and Halalii as described in the next-to-last paragraph of Trip H5. (I've chosen this spur trail because it offers such a stunning view of Ka Moa o Pele's vent as you walk it this direction.)

On the saddle, go right on the spur trail that heads around the east side of Halalii—uninteresting until it meets the Halemauu Trail on the saddle between Halalii and Puu Naue at Kawilinau in "Pele's Paint Pot. Turn left (west) on the Halemauu Trail through the dazzling colors of Pele's Paint Pot and follow it west and then northwest to the Silversword Loop, reversing part of the description of Trip H5. You can pick up the Silversword Loop now or on your way back from Holua Cabin/Campground. Continue northwest, still reversing Trip H5's description, to Holua Cabin/Campground. The scenery opens westward before you, and the meadow below Holua Cabin contrasts sharply with the forbidding lava wilderness you're traversing.

After enjoying your lunch at beautiful Holua Cabin, retrace your steps to the junction where the Halemauu Trail turns left (east) toward Pele's Paint Pot. Here, you bear right, past Pele's Pig Pen. At the junction just beyond Pele's Pig Pen, you turn sharply right and begin climbing the northern slopes of Ka Moa o Pele to a saddle between it and an unnamed cone to its north. Enjoy the view from this saddle before descending west and then southwest on the red slopes of Ka Moa o Pele. The dark brown slopes of Puu o Maui rise on your right (west). As the trail levels out, you enter a choppy, frozen "sea" of lava whose stony waves have crests of gray and orange rock and troughs of black sand.

You leave the lava "sea" behind as you approach a junction with the Sliding Sands Trail, where bracken, *mamane*, and yellow-flowered, alien evening primrose grow. At this junction, turn left (east) onto the Sliding Sands Trail and follow it back to Kapalaoa Cabin as described in Trip H13 to end a satisfying and highly varied hike.

Ideally....

Ideally you'd stay two nights at Kapalaoa Cabin to enjoy this side trip at a leisurely pace. If you can't get a permit for two nights, an alternative is to get an early start, stash most of your gear at Kapalaoa Cabin, take this side trip with a day-pack, and pack out when you get back to Kapalaoa Cabin—before the next party arrives, you hope. Another choice, if you can get the necessary permit, is a backpacking variation on Trip H16: backpack down the Sliding Sands Trail as far as Kapalaoa Cabin, take one of these lovely spur trails to Holua Cabin/Campground (where you'll stay), and then pack out on the Halemauu Trail. However you manage it, I hope you won't miss the beauty of the central crater.

Trip H15

Sliding Sands Trail to Paliku Cabin/Campground

Distance	Elevation gain	Hiking time	Topos
19½ miles	3400' (Loss/gain)	15–16 hours (over 2 days)	Kilohana 7½', Nahiku 7½'

Difficulty: Strenuous, hiking boots strongly recommended

Highlights: The beauty of the Sliding Sands Trail is yours to enjoy until, at Olii Puu, you pick up the Halemauu Trail for the different, but equally beautiful, stretch to Paliku Cabin/Campground.

Driving instructions: Follow the driving instructions of Trip H9.

Trip H15 continues next page

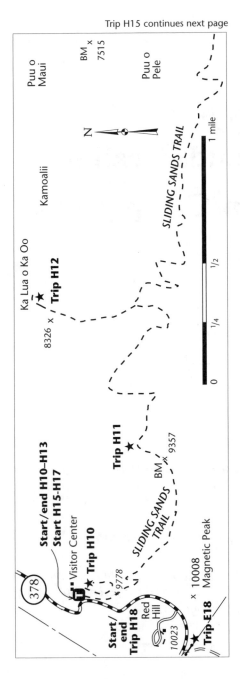

Permit/permission required: Required for an overnight stay at Kapalaoa or Paliku Cabin or both (by reservation only) or at the campground adjacent to Paliku Cabin; see suggestions at the end of this trip and details in Appendix A.

Description (strenuous trip):

Day 1 (9¾ miles): Follow Trip H13 to Kapalaoa Cabin. On this trip, you can skip the detour to Ka Lua o Ka Oo (add just under 1 mile out and back and 150' elevation gain if you're determined to see it).

After a rest on Kapalaoa Cabin's lawn, you continue east on the Sliding Sands Trail into scrub country, where you soon begin a gentle descent as the trail bears northeast. Puu Maile, visible to the northeast when you left Kapalaoa, is soon hidden by a ridge of *aa*, and there's a dry wash to the southeast. The trail presently levels out amid rocks some of which are a lovely soft, dark, pinkish-red color. The trail becomes dusty as it passes through more scrub and bracken.

It's not long before Oili Puu comes into view ahead

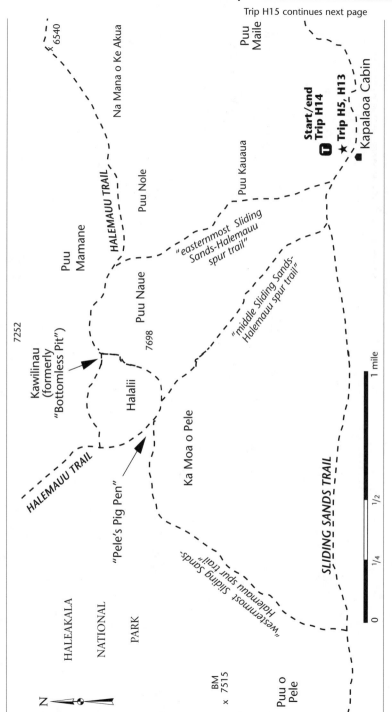

Trip H15 continues next page

Puu Maile

Start/end
Trip H14

Trip H5, H13

Kapalaoa Cabin

6540

Na Mana o Ke Akua

Puu Kauaua

HALEMAUU TRAIL

Puu Nole

"easternmost Sliding
Sands-Halemauu
spur trail"

Puu Mamane

"middle Sliding Sands-
Halemauu spur trail"

7252

Puu Naue

Kawilinau
(formerly
"Bottomless Pit")

7698

Halalii

HALEMAUU TRAIL

Ka Moa o Pele

"Pele's Pig Pen"

SLIDING SANDS TRAIL

"westernmost Sliding Sands-
Halemauu spur trail"

HALEAKALA

NATIONAL

PARK

N

BM
x 7515

Puu o
Pele

0   1/4   1/2   1 mile

Trip H15 continued from previous page

Maui Trails

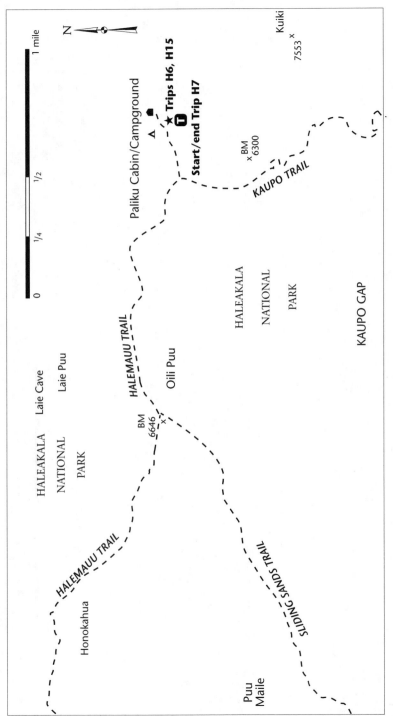

N

1 mile

1/2

1/4

0

Kuiki
7553 ×

Paliku Cabin/Campground

Trips H6, H15

Start/end Trip H7

× BM
6300

KAUPO TRAIL

HALEAKALA

NATIONAL

PARK

KAUPO GAP

Laie Cave

Laie Puu

HALEAKALA

NATIONAL

PARK

HALEMAUU TRAIL

Oili Puu

BM
6646 ×

HALEMAUU TRAIL

SLIDING SANDS TRAIL

Honokahua

Puu
Maile

266

Trip H15 continued from previous page

to the northeast as you descend moderately to steeply on a very rough, rocky, loose track and through a region of scrub and jagged vents. A few curious little "buttes" stand a few feet above the general terrain here. A couple of them seem to be the products of spatter lava, but one, standing north of the trail and isolated in a flow of *pahoehoe*, appears to be a tiny columnar basalt formation (see Trip E9 for a discussion of this type of formation).

Your descent becomes more gradual, but it is still quite rough, as Paliku's meadow becomes visible to the east, only to be hidden by Oili Puu as you begin crossing a broad lava field. Ridges of *aa* are separated by narrow channels of green scrub—mostly *aalii, ohelo,* and *pukiawe*. Kaupo Gap opens on your right (east), but the challenge of negotiating the loose *aa* may keep you from appreciating it.

You leave the lava field on cinders dotted by *pukiawe* and evening primrose and shortly reach the junction of the Halemauu and Sliding Sands trails. Turn right (northeast) here around the base of scrub-covered Oili Puu and follow Trip H6 to Paliku Cabin/Campground.

Day 2 (9¾ miles): Retrace your steps to the Sliding Sands trailhead.

Logistics: The easier way to do this trip is to stay a night at Kapalaoa Cabin. If you want to stay overnight at Kapalaoa Cabin and can get a reservation for it, your trip will probably be easier if you backpack in directly to Paliku Cabin/Campground (downhill) and then stay at Kapalaoa Cabin on your way out (uphill).

Trip H16

Sliding Sands Trail to Halemauu Trail Adventure

Distance	Elevation gain	Hiking time	Topos
13 miles	1680' (Loss/gain)	7–8 hours	Kilohana 7½', Nahiku 7½'

Difficulty: *Strenuous, hiking boots strongly recommended*

Highlights: *This is, I believe, the single finest dayhike in Haleakala's crater—make that the single finest dayhike on Maui. It's as complete a crater adventure as you can enjoy without staying overnight in the crater. By all means allow time for detours to Ka Lua o Ka Oo, Kawilinau and Pele's Paint Pot, and the Silversword Loop! Take plenty of color film, and budget your time so that you can take advantage of the multitude of photo opportunities along the way.*

Driving instructions: This trip is a shuttle, so leave one car at the Halemauu Trail by following the driving instructions of Trip H3. Then, following the driving instructions of Trip H10, drive to White Hill to start your adventure at the Sliding Sands Trail.

Permit/permission required: None if done as a dayhike. See Appendix A for information on cabins and camping in the crater.

Description: Follow Trip H13 down the Sliding Sands Trail, detouring to visit Ka Lua o Ka Oo, to the junction with the first of the three maintained spur trails to the Halemauu Trail, 4¾ miles including the detour. Here, with Puu o Pele above you to the west and with Ka Moa o Pele ahead of you to the northeast, you turn left (northeast) onto the spur trail through the bracken, *mamane*, and evening primrose that grow around this junction.

Follow the spur trail northeast and then east, reversing part of Trip H14, through the choppy lava "sea" and up the red slopes of Ka Moa o Pele. You descend to the point just east of and above Pele's Pig Pen on the saddle between Ka Moa o Pele and Halalii. Turn right

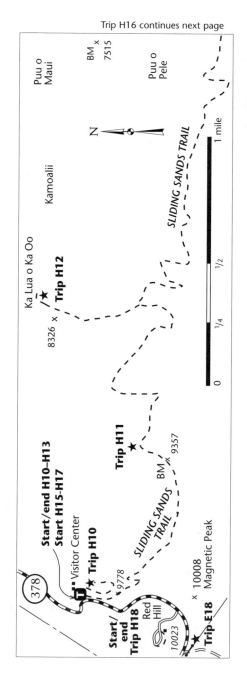

Trip H16 continues next page

Trip H16 continues next page

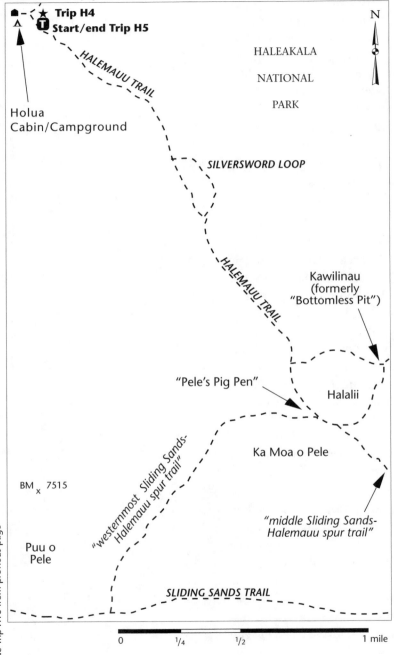

Continue Trip H16 from previous page

Continue Trip H16 from previous page

and follow the trail around Halalii, going left at the next junction, to Kawilinau. Turn left (west) onto the Halemauu Trail at Kawilinau for a short walk through the intensely colorful area called Pele's Paint Pot.

At the next junction, on the west side of Halalii, you turn right (northwest) toward the Silversword Loop and Holua Cabin/Campground. Now you reverse the steps of part of Trip H5, detouring to see the Silversword Loop if you wish. The amount of vegetation increases as you rise toward Holua Cabin/Campground, where you'll welcome a chance to rest. This area seems especially green and flourishing after the colorful but barren regions of the crater you've been traveling through since leaving White Hill. All too soon, the pressure of time obliges you to resume your trip, reversing the steps of Trip H4 down the ridge, across the meadow, and up Leleiwi Pali to the crater rim.

At the crater rim viewpoint that's the destination for Trips H2 and H3, you can't help but pause for one final, long look at the stupendous world of Haleakala's crater. Continuing, you now enjoy views downslope to East Maui's north coast on your way to the Halemauu trailhead and your shuttle car. At last you can shed your pack, change into tennies, and ease your weary body into a soft car seat.

Sure, you're tired. But what's being tired compared to being dazzled by Haleakala's splendors?!

Shuttle, anyone?

How do you set up a shuttle for a group that's sharing just one rental car? It's easy if you've made sure your group includes at least one non-hiker who doesn't mind driving the hikers around. Perhaps that's not so easy. Other options: rent another car for the necessary period; take the trip with an organized group whose arrangements include the shuttle; or, if you have friends on Maui, arrange for one of them to pick you up.

But let's assume you're limited to one car and have no other options. What if everyone wants to hike? What if there's only the one of you? The classic solution is to leave your car at the Halemauu Trailhead and hitchhike to White Hill and the Sliding Sands Trailhead. The Halemauu Trailhead, on a hairpin curve of the main road, lacks a safe place for uphill hitchhikers to stand and for a car to pull over. However, a little footpath leads across the hairpin and down to a wide turnout. If your upraised thumb doesn't get you a ride, try flourishing a $20 bill next to it.

Or forget taking that trip as a shuttle. Instead, select a midpoint along the trip and take an out-and-back hike from each end of it to your midpoint. This has some real advantages: You get to enjoy the trip twice as much; you won't have to make any complicated arrangements; you won't have to hold yourself to a schedule for meeting a ride; and you won't keep anyone waiting and worrying at the other end.

Backpack It!

While this trip is described as a dayhike, you can also do it as a backpack if you can get permission to stay at Holua Cabin/Campground.

Trip H17

Grand Crater Tour
Backpack

Distance	Elevation gain	Hiking time	Topos
Just over 20 miles	2120' (Loss/gain)	15–16 hours (over 3–4 days)	Kilohana, 7½' Nahiku 7½'

Trail map: Day 1: Begins on the maps for Trip H13, pages 256-257; day 2: continues on the maps for Trip H15, pages 265-266; day 3: continues on the maps for Trip H6, pages 228-230; day 4: ends on the map for Trip H4, page 214.

Difficulty: Strenuous, hiking boots strongly recommended

Highlights: You see virtually every one of the finest crater features that maintained trails take you to. On the way, you sample the comforts of the cabins or campgrounds, or both, depending on the mix of reserva-

tions and permits you're able to get. The easiest trip, described below, is possible only if you can get a reservation for Kapalaoa Cabin for your first night. Otherwise, combine Days 1 and 2 to go directly to Paliku Cabin/- Campground on your Day 1 as described in Trip H15, and consider spending two nights at Paliku Cabin/Campground. That would allow you to take Trip H7, too.

Driving instructions: This trip is a shuttle like Trip H16, whose driving instructions you should follow.

Permit/permission required: Required for an overnight stay at any of the cabins (by reservation only) or at the campgrounds adjacent to Paliku and Holua cabins; see Appendix A.

Overview map

*Formerly "Bottomless Pit"

Description (easiest trip):

Day 1 (just over 5¾ miles): Follow Trip H13 from the Sliding Sands trailhead to Kapalaoa Cabin.

Day 2 (4 miles): Follow Trip H15 from Kapalaoa Cabin to Paliku Cabin/Campground.

Day 3 (6½ miles): Reverse the steps of Day 2 of Trip H6 from Paliku Cabin/Campground to Holua Cabin/Campground.

Day 4 (just under 4 miles): Reverse the steps of Trip H4 from Holua Cabin/Campground to the Halemauu trailhead. Early birds will find that it's possible to take Trip H5 before packing out.

Trip H18

Red Hill Mini-hike

Distance	Elevation gain	Hiking time	Topos
Negligible	23′	Negligible	*Kilohana 7½′* (Optional)

Difficulty: *Very easy, tennis shoes recommended*

Highlights: *Red Hill (Puu Ulaula), 10,023 feet high, is the highest point on Haleakala and, therefore, on Maui. The parking lot itself is at 10,000 feet! The views from Red Hill are superb. The air is pretty thin at this altitude, so take it easy. Make this an early morning visit so that the cloud bank that normally forms by midmorning won't obstruct your view.*

Driving instructions: Follow the driving instructions of Trip H10 past the Visitor Center turnoff at White Hill and continue all the way up Highway 378 past the turnoff to Science City to the parking lot for the observation shelter at the very top of Haleakala.

Permit/permission required: None.

Description: From the parking lot, climb the stairs to the enclosed observation shelter, where marked stations point out features of the nearly-360° view from here. Mauna Kea and Mauna Loa on the Big Island of Hawaii, many miles away to the south-southeast, are particularly striking from Red Hill. Magnetic Peak, right next door in the southeast, is reputed to be so full of iron that it interferes with compass readings.

In a hundred paces away from the observation shelter toward Science City, veer left onto a rock-bordered dirt path for more great views from the other side of Red Hill. Curve around the edge of this cinder cone for about 150 paces to its summit, then zigzag down to the parking lot, which is in the cone's crater.

From here, take the other stairs down to the parking lot and return to your car.

Science City

Science City

The view southwest and west over Science City, the Isthmus, and West Maui is unparalleled. The sight of Science City is even more striking from outside the shelter, so follow the little paved path outside the shelter.

The white domes and buildings of Science City and the barren red-brown clinker of Haleakala's summit region combine to make a landscape so stark, so surreal, and so alien that you may think you've strayed onto the set of a science-fiction movie or been translated to Mars like Edgar Rice Burroughs's hero John Carter.

ALERT: Please don't step off the path. Despite its apparent lifelessness, there is life in this harsh environment, and a careless step can too easily crush seedlings and tiny creatures hidden in the clinker.

Skyline Trail

Remember that you can reverse the directions for the Skyline Trail, Trip E18 in this book, and take it from Science City, just below Red Hill. That will make it an upside-down trip, but getting to the Skyline Trail from Science City rather than from Polipoli will be more practical for many people, because the road to Polipoli is awful, while the road to Red Hill is quite good.

Your best bet is probably to leave your car parked here at Red Hill and carefully walk back down the road to the turnoff for Science City. The Skyline Trail branches off from the Science City road just a little past the National Park boundary sign. This would add ¾ mile and 100 feet of elevation gain to your Skyline Trail hike or mountain-bicycle trip. You could more than compensate for that by turning around at Ballpark Junction instead of going all the way to Polipoli. Sturdy cyclists who can set up the shuttle may be interested in continuing all the way down from Polipoli to Highway 377 and meeting their shuttle ride in Kula.

Bibliography

Beckwith, Martha. *Hawaiian Mythology.* New Haven: Yale University Press (for the Folklore Foundation of Vassar College), 1940. Reprint. Honolulu: University of Hawaii Press, 1970, 1976.

Bisignani, J.D. *Hawaii Handbook.* 2nd ed. Chico, California: Moon Publications, Inc., 1989.

Carlquist, Sherwin. *Hawaii, A Natural History.* 2nd ed., 2nd printing. Lawai, Kauai: National [formerly Pacific] Tropical Botanical Garden, 1980, 1985.

Chisolm, Craig. *Hawaiian Hiking Trails.* 3rd ed. Lake Oswego, Oregon: The Fernglen Press, 1989.

Clark, John. *Hawaii's Secret Beaches, A Guide to Twenty-Four Hawaiian Beaches.* Honolulu: Tongg Publishing, 1989.

Day, A. Grove, and Carl Stroven, Eds. *A Hawaiian Reader.* Appleton-Century-Crofts, 1959. Reprint. Honolulu: Mutual Publishing Company, 1984.

Day, A. Grove. *Hawaii and Its People.* New York: Duell, Sloan and Pearce, 1955.

Epidemiology Branch, State Department of Health, State of Hawaii. "Leptospirosis in Hawaii." October 1, 1987.

Fleming, Martha Foss. *Old Trails of Maui.* Sponsored by William & Mary Alexander Chapter, Daughters of the American Revolution, 1933. (Obtained through the courtesy of Mr. Don Reeser, Superintendent, Haleakala National Park.)

Hargreaves, Dorothy, and Bob Hargreaves. *Hawaii Blossoms.* Japan: Dorothy and Bob Hargreaves, 1958. Reprint. Lahaina: Ross-Hargreaves.

——. *Tropical Trees of Hawaii.* Kailua: Hargreaves Company.

Hawai'i Audubon Society. *Hawaii's Birds.* 4th ed. Honolulu: Hawai'i Audubon Society, 1989.

Hill, Mary. *Geology of the Sierra Nevada.* Berkeley: University of California Press, 1975.

Joesting, Edward. *Hawaii, An Uncommon History.* New York: W.W. Norton & Company Inc., 1972.

Kepler, Angela Kay. *Maui's Hana Highway, A Visitor's Guide.* Honolulu: Mutual Publishing Company, 1987.

Kepler, Cameron B., and Angela Kay Kepler. *Haleakala: A Guide to the Mountain.* Honolulu: Mutual Publishing Company, 1988.

Kirch, Patrick Vinton. *Feathered Gods and Fishhooks: An Introduction to Hawaiian Archaeology and Prehistory.* Honolulu: University of Hawaii Press, 1985.

Kyselka, Will, and Ray Lanterman. *Maui: How It Came To Be.* Honolulu: University of Hawaii Press, 1980.

Levi, Herbert W., and Lorna R. Levi. *Spiders and their Kin.* New York: Golden Press, 1987.

Macdonald, Gordon A., Agatin T. Abbott, and Frank L. Peterson. *Volcanoes in the Sea, the Geology of Hawaii.* 2nd ed. Honolulu: University of Hawaii Press, 1986.

Mack, Jim. *Haleakala: the Story Behind the Scenery.* 4th printing. Las Vegas: KC Publications, 1979.

Merlin, Mark David. *Hawaiian Coastal Plants and Scenic Shorelines.* 3rd printing. Honolulu: Oriental Publishing Co., 1986.

——. *Hawaiian Forest Plants.* 3rd ed. Honolulu: The Oriental Publishing Co., 1980.

Mrantz, Maxine. *Women of Old Hawaii.* Honolulu: Aloha Publishing, 1975.

Pukui, Mary Kawena, Samuel H. Elbert, and Esther T. Mookini. *The Pocket Hawaiian Dictionary.* Honolulu: University of Hawaii Press, 1975.

Smith, Rodney N. *Hawaii: A Walker's Guide.* 2nd ed. Edison, New Jersey: Hunter Publishing, Inc., 1998.

Sohmer, S.H., and R. Gustafson. *Plants and Flowers of Hawai'i.* Honolulu: University of Hawaii Press, 1987.

Winnett, Thomas, and Melanie Findling. *Backpacking Basics.* 3rd ed. Berkeley: Wilderness Press, 1988.

Woolliams, Keith. *A Guide to Hawaii's Popular Trees.* 2nd ed. Aiea, Hawaii: Island Heritage Publishing, 1988.

Appendix A.
Camping on Maui

Backcountry camping accessible on foot

Backcountry camping that's accessible only on foot is practical for the tourist from the mainland only in Haleakala crater (Haleakala National Park). You must have a permit to stay in the campgrounds or cabins in the crater. You may not camp in the crater outside of the campgrounds or cabins. Your stay in the crater is limited to 3 nights per month, whether in cabins or campgrounds or a combination of cabins and campgrounds. Your stay at any one location in the crater is limited to 2 consecutive nights; for this purpose, a cabin and its adjacent campground (if any) count as different locations.

Crater campgrounds

There are two tent-campgrounds in the crater, one near Holua Cabin (6960') and the other near Paliku Cabin (6380'). Permits for tent camping in the crater are issued only in person at Park Headquarters (or, for very early starts before Park Headquarters opens, at the Visitor Center near the summit) and only on the day you begin your trip. There are quotas, so be prepared to modify your itinerary or come back another day if the quotas are filled. There is no fee. The crater can be cold (my thermometer read 40°F one clear morning after a rainy night at Holua Campground), windy, and rainy, so you must be prepared with a rainproof tent, warm clothes, rain gear, and a stove that you can start and keep going in wind and rain. A friend who thought he wouldn't need his whole tent in Hawaii and who went into Haleakala crater with only the rainfly for shelter was very cold, very soggy, and very sorry. The ranger who issues your permit will ask about your preparedness.

Crater cabins

There are three cabins in Haleakala Crater: Holua Cabin, Kapalaoa Cabin, and Paliku Cabin. Only one party as a unit may use a cabin at a time; a cabin holds up to 12 people. The cabins have tables, benches, bare bunkbeds (you'll still need your sleeping bag), and a kitchen with potable running water, a wood stove and wood (or those logs made from chips), and cooking and eating utensils. There is no electricity or lanterns; bring your flashlight and candle lantern. Each cabin also has an outhouse. Applying for a cabin is complicated; write the Park Superintendent (address below) to find out what the latest procedure is for applying. Applying doesn't guarantee you'll get to rent a cabin. Who actually gets to rent a cabin is decided by lottery; you'll be notified of the results. *Get your information and start the application process early!*

People sometimes cancel their cabin reservations on the spur of the moment. It's remotely possible that you'll get a night at a cabin just because you happen to be at the Park Headquarters counter when someone cancels a reservation. Don't count on it, though.

Haleakala National Park's address is:
Haleakala National Park
Box 369
Makawao, Maui, HI 96768
(808) 572-7749 (recording of general information)
(808) 572-9177
    (recording of camping and cabin information)
(808) 572-9306
    (park headquarters; 7:30 A.M. to 4:00 P.M.
    Hawaii Standard Time)
www.nps.gov/hale/

Other (outside Haleakala)

There are two other possibilities for those who are desperate to do some backpacking, though these sites are also accessible by 4WD vehicles. See the supplemental information following Trips E17 and E19.

Car camping

Maui doesn't offer much car camping—the kind of camping where you drive up, pay your bucks, pick a space, park your car, and pitch your tent there and live out of it (or live out of your parked vehicle). For those who enjoy car camping, there is a list below of the places you can car camp on Maui. This information is largely from other sources, such as the agency in charge; I've verified the information for only a couple of these places.

Car camping at Haleakala National Park
Car camping at Haleakala National Park is limited to Hosmer Grove (just off Highway 378, which goes to Haleakala crater's principal trailheads and to Haleakala's summit) and Kipahulu (the coastal section of the park, south and west of Hana). No permit is required. Camping is free. Camping at Hosmer Grove is limited to 25 persons (organized groups are limited to 15 persons). However, there may be no one to see that the limit is observed. The result may be that Hosmer Grove, so peaceful by day, will be jammed full of people by nightfall. Those who can't cram into the campground may try to sleep in their cars along the road! A stay at Hosmer Grove may be less than idyllic. Camping at Hosmer Grove and Kipahulu is limited to 3 nights per month. Trailers are permitted in the parking lot of Hosmer Grove. RVs are not permitted at either site.

Car camping at the state parks
Car camping at the state parks is by permit only and for a maximum of 5 consecutive nights in any 30-day period. Permits are free. They are issued Monday through Friday, 8 A.M. to 4 P.M., at the Division of State Parks office in Wailuku. The person appearing to apply for the permit must provide proper identification for each person in the party who is 18 years old or older. "Proper identification" means a driver's license or passport. You may also apply by mail at least seven days in advance of your proposed trip by writing to the Division of State Parks. When applying by mail, include a copy of the proper identification for each person in the party who is 18 years old or older. Trailers and RVs are not permitted in Maui's state parks. For the state parks, write or call:

> Department of Land and Natural Resources
> Division of State Parks, Maui District
> P.O. Box 1049, 54 S. High St.
> Wailuku, Maui, HI 96793
> (808) 984-8109

Car camping on Division of Forestry and Wildlife lands

At present, there are no car-campgrounds in areas managed by the Division of Forestry and Wildlife.

Car camping at Maui County's parks

Two of Maui County's parks allow car camping. It's limited to a maximum of 3 consecutive nights at one campsite. Permits are required. There is a fee per night. Obtain permits by mail from:

> Department of Parks and Recreation, County of Maui
> 1580 Kaahumanu Avenue
> Wailuku, Maui, Hawaii 96793
> (808) 243-7389

Car camping on West Maui

As of this writing, private Camp Pecusa (below) offers the only car camping on West Maui. However, a public car-campground is in the planning stage for West Maui. Look for news of it when you get your packets of information from Maui's public agencies.

Private

Car camping is possible at a private campground, Camp Pecusa. This is an Episopalian Church campground on the beach at Olowalu, but they allow the general public to camp there for a fee as long as there's room. Write or call:

> Camp Pecusa
> 800 Olowalu Village
> Lahaina, Maui, HI 96761
> (808) 661-4303

Car Camping Opportunities

Name	Type	Nearest Town	Amenities; Restrictions
Hosmer Grove	National Park	Kula	Grills, tables, potable water, picnic pavilion, toilets. Tents only in campground proper; trailers permitted in parking lot. Rainy. Free. No permit required. Stays limited. At 6800'.
Kipahulu	National Park	Hana	Grills, toilets, and tables. No potable water. Tents only. Free. No permit required. Stays limited. Near sea level.
Waianapanapa	State	Hana	Potable water, picnic tables, outdoor showers, barbecue grills, toilets. Tents or campers. Free. Permit required. Stays limited. Near sea level.
Kaumahina	State	Between Paia and Hana but not near anything	Restrooms, picnic tables, outdoor grills. Off Hana Highway in rain forest; no beach. Free. Permit re-quired. Stays limited. Near sea level.
Polipoli	State	About an hour from Kula, Waiakoa	Potable water, rest-room, picnic tables, shelters. Tents only. Dark and rainy. Free. Permit required. Stays limited. At 6200'.

Car Camping Opportunities continued

Name	Type	Nearest Town	Amenities; Restrictions
H.A. Baldwin	County	Paia	Restrooms and outdoor showers. Tents only. Fee. Permit required; see above. The camping area abuts the highway. Stays limited. Sea level.
Rainbow Park	County	Paia	Restrooms. Tents only. Fee. Permit required; see above. Stays limited. Elevation unspecified; estimated at 800'.
Camp Pecusa	Private	Olowalu	Fee. No limit on stays. Sea level.
Kanaha Beach Park	County	Kahalui	Permit required. Fee. Curfew. 3-day limit per site. North side of isthmus. Sea level.
Windmill Beach	Private	Kapalua	Permit required. Fee. 3-day limit. Open beach; no facilities. Sea level.

Cabins

The following areas offer cabins, which you should reserve (or try to reserve) months in advance.

Haleakala National Park

There are three backcountry cabins in Haleakala National Park in the crater. See "Backcountry camping accessible on foot" at the front of this section.

State parks

There are 12 cabins at Waianapanapa State Park (very popular) and one cabin at Polipoli State Park (popular). There is a fee per person per night, and your stay is limited to a maximum of 5 consecutive nights in any 30-day period. Write or call the state parks at the address or telephone number given above. I think the trail shelters in Polipoli are not worthy of your consideration; see the note following Trip E15.

Private

Camp Pecusa also has a few cabins, for which they charge a modest fee. Write the camp at the address given above or call the telephone number also given above.

Appendix B.
Hikes You Won't Find Here and Why

You may have read articles on the following hikes, seen them mentioned in other books, or noticed them on topos. Some are in this book under different names. Some are closed because landowners no longer give permission to hike them. Others have become unsafe; don't let your vacation end in the emergency room! Finally, I judged that some are too remote and boring to be worth your time.

West Maui/Isthmus

Iao Valley State Park—Poohahoahoa, Nakalaloa, and Kinihapai streams

A spur trail that went partway up Poohahoahoa Stream and was formerly Trip W9 is now closed. The rest of these streams are trail-less; reputed to be difficult, rugged, and slippery where you have to walk in the streambed; subject to flash flooding.

Tableland Trail: Now closed.

Lahaina "L," David Malo's grave

Pioneer Mill Company no longer allows hikers to cross their land, so this viewful hike is no longer possible. Formerly Trip W11.

Puu Kukui

Closed to casual hikers. The Nature Conservancy now helps the landowner, the Maui Land and Pineapple Company, manage the swamps on the slopes and summit of Puu Kukui. Access is severely restricted to protect rare native species, the ecosystem, and the watershed. The survival of endangered species and fragile ecosystems is much more important than the recreational wishes of our numerous and mobile species. We can so easily go somewhere else to hike—and just about anywhere else sounds better than Puu Kukui, anyway. One source describes Puu Kukui as having been "the most exhilarating and interesting" hike on Maui and describes the hiker's condition on this trail as "...soaked to the skin and chilled to the bone." Okay, all of you who came to Maui to get soaked to the skin and chilled to the bone, raise your hands!...That's what I thought. (Apparently, the reason for going to the top of Puu Kukui was to enjoy the views—views seldom available because of the cloud cover.)

Cross Above Wailuku
Wailuku Agribusiness no longer grants permission to hike to this landmark.

Huluhulupueo Stream
The bridge described as the starting point is over the Waihee River. Huluhulupueo Stream is a tributary of the Waihee River, joining it over a mile upriver from the bridge. I found no parking on or near the bridge. Access to the river from the bridge and highway is blocked by barbed wire, KEEP OUT signs, somebody's yard, and steep concrete abutments.

East Maui (except for Haleakala National Park, which you'll find below)

Twin Falls
Formerly Trip E1 in this book and sometimes found in other books, this area is private property on both sides of the highway, and the owner doesn't want us hiking on it. The owner tries to keep the land posted, but the NO TRESPASSING signs are frequently vandalized, often missing. Vandalizing of cars parked around here is a serious problem.

Keanae Village
With all due respect to Keanae, the village isn't particularly interesting. I found a NO TRESPASSING sign between me and the one thing I thought might have been interesting. Also, if the people of Keanae

wanted to make a tourist showplace of their village, there'd be signs on the highway inviting us to come on down and visit—but there aren't. There's a restroom near the end of the peninsula, and you might want to take some photos of the coast from there. That's about it.

Blue Pool

See Trip E4, Ulaino Road.

Hana Town

Hana isn't a particularly good "walking" town, as explained in Trip E10, because it's hilly, hot and humid, and lacks sidewalks. See Trip E10 for a walk in Hana.

Red-Cinder Beach

Formerly Trip E12 in this book. The unmaintained path to the red-cinder beach has suffered enough erosion that I think it is no longer safe for most hikers. The footing on the steep part is terrible because of loose cinders and other rubble, and the steep part has become very narrow as material has sloughed off the cinder cone here. (Recall that the landslide that made Kaahumanu's birthplace inaccessible is just on the other side of this cone.) A fall from this part of the path would surely lead to grave injury, maybe to death.

Helio's Grave

Trail reportedly too dangerous to hike any more.

Polipoli State Park

With all due respect to the people of Maui, there is little at Polipoli State Park for the visitor from the mainland. About specific trails, alphabetically:

Boundary Trail: An oppressive, dark, and very dull trail made irritatingly hard to follow by the number of thoughtless use trails that crisscross it. Northeastern part damaged by pigs and dirt bikes.

Haleakala Ridge Trail: Crisscrossed by use trails; dull. See Polipoli Loop, below.

Kahua Road: Worthwhile. See Trip E17.

Mamane Trail: Under construction but must be shared with mountain bikers—ugh! See Trip E18.

Plum Trail: Oppressive, dark, and dull. The plum trees have died from lack of light and from competition. See Polipoli Loop, below.

Polipoli Loop (Polipoli, Haleakala Ridge, Plum, and Redwood trails): This hike is an old standard, but I found it oppressive, dark, and dull. Here's a condensed description of it in case you have a lot of time to kill: Loop; moderate; tennis shoes okay; mountains, 3½ miles, 880' elevation gain (upside-down trip), 1¾ hours. This hike starts on the Polipoli Trail near the west edge of the campground. You leave the campground on that trail, under oppressive overgrowth, climb steeply but briefly to a 3-way junction, and turn right (west) onto what turns out to be the Haleakala Ridge Trail. The trail presently turns into the Plum Trail, which you follow past an intersection with the Tie Trail and past the abandoned Civilian Conservation Corps bunkhouse to a junction with the Boundary and Redwood trails. Turn right on the Redwood Trail and reverse the steps of Trip E16 back to the campground. You may want to take the Boundary Trail to the Fuchsia Wall before turning onto the Redwood Trail.

Polipoli Trail: Oppressive, dark, and dull. See Polipoli Loop, above.

Redwood Trail: Oppressive, dark, and dull. Unlike any mainland stand of coast redwoods I've ever seen—and not a change for the better. See Trip E16 and Polipoli Loop, above.

Skyline Trail: Worthwhile. See Trip E18.

Tie Trail: Oppressive, dark, and dull.

Upper Waiakoa (Waiohuli) Trail: Severely damaged by feral pigs; may be impassable.

Waiakoa Loop Trail: Badly damaged by feral pigs; may be impassable.

Puu Pimoe

Ulupalakua Ranch no longer gives permission to hike here.

Piiholo Hill

Haleakala Ranch no longer gives permission to hike here (they've leased it to another party who doesn't give permission, either).

Haleakala National Park

This book covers all the *maintained* trails in Haleakala National Park as Trips H1 through H18. A number of trails that used to be maintained aren't any more and should be considered unsafe. Particularly in the western part of the crater, the maintained trails represent the only environmentally safe way through a very fragile ecosystem. Safety—yours and the ecosystem's—dictates that you stick to the maintained trails. There are more than enough maintained trails in and around Haleakala to keep you busy, including enough crater trails to keep you hopping for the maximum 3 nights/4 days you can spend in the crater.

Appendix C.
How I Got Distances, Elevations, Times, and Trail Maps

I estimated distances primarily by time, knowing that I hike 2 miles/hour and backpack at 1⅓ miles/hour. I compared the distances I got by time with distance values supplied by the agencies in charge of the trails. In a few cases, I also had distance data from plots I'd made from the topos. When those distances were close, I felt satisfied with the distance I'd estimated by time. I usually rounded the distances off to the nearest ¼ or ⅓ mile.

I got most driving distances by rental-car odometer, which was consistent to within ±¹⁄₁₀ mile over routes I drove repeatedly. When I had not started from Wailuku, I added or subtracted the distance from my starting point to Wailuku. I found that in a some cases I did not get usable odometer data; in those cases, I used data from the University of Hawaii Press map of Maui.

I determined elevation from topos and with an altimeter. Where I had altimeter data, I looked for close correspondence between those values, topo values, and any values supplied by the agency in charge of the trail.

Trail times are based on the time I actually spent in motion on the trail.

I made the original digital trail maps by first scanning relevant pieces of the USGS topos into a computer. I put the resulting digitized topo information that applied to a trip or a set of trips into the bottom layer of a multiple-layer electronic drawing. I then traced selected topo information onto transparent electronic upper layers. I deleted the scanned data before I saved out the finished maps in a format compatible with the desktop publishing program used to lay out this book. I left out the elevation contours because they would have taken me too long to draw and because they would have made these grayscale maps too busy. I added, deleted, or modified topo information that I knew had changed. My choices of conventions for trails, roads, boundaries, etc., primarily reflect the capability of the software I originally used to create the maps.

Many trails on Maui do not appear at all on the topos or in usable form on any official agency map. For them, I approximated the route based on field notes and sketches and any agency information I could find.

The maps, as well as the layout of the book, have been completely overhauled and reworked for the third edition by Wilderness Press. You'll find improved and clarified map conventions, new icons and design elements, as well as new photographs in this edition.

Index

Hawaii Books from Wilderness Press

Hawaii Trails
Walks, strolls, and treks on the Big Island
Choose from 60 of the finest walks on the Big Island, including those in Mauna Loa, Kilauea, Kaumana caves, and Mauna Kea State Park.
ISBN 0-89997-311-6

Kauai Trails
Walks, strolls, and treks on the Garden Island
The Garden Isle is paradise for walkers, and this guidebok describes 59 the best hikes, from Hanalei Bay to Waimea Canyon, from Wailue Falls t the Na Pali Coast.
ISBN 0-89997-305-1

Maui Trails
Walks, strolls, and treks on the Valley Island
Discover 52 walking trips in the Valley Island, from 1 hour to 3 days, in Iao Valley and Polipoli state parks, Waihee Valley and the crater at Haleakala.
ISBN 0-89997-323X

Oahu Trails
Walks, strolls, and treks on the Capital Isle
Escapte Waikiki and discover the beaches, cliffs, and inland rainforests c Oahu's less populated areas with 45 of the best walking tours on the island.
ISBN 0-89997-245-4

For ordering information, contact your local bookseller or Wilderness Press, www.wildernesspress.co